STUDIES ON ETHNIC GROUPS IN CHINA

Stevan Harrell, Editor

# In the Land of the Eastern Queendom

*The Politics of Gender and Ethnicity on the*

*Sino-Tibetan Border*

\*

TENZIN JINBA

UNIVERSITY OF WASHINGTON PRESS / SEATTLE AND LONDON

Material from chapter 4 appears in *Modern China* 39, no. 5 (September 2013). Material from chapter 5 appears in *China Quarterly* (forthcoming).

© 2014 by the University of Washington Press
Printed and bound in the United States of America
Composed in Minion, a typeface designed by Robert Slimbach
17 16 15 14 13  5 4 3 2 1

University of Washington Press
PO Box 50096, Seattle, WA 98145, USA
www.washington.edu / uwpress

Library of Congress Cataloging-in-Publication Data
Tenzin, Jinba.
In the land of the eastern queendom : the politics of gender and ethnicity on the Sino-Tibetan border / Tenzin Jinba. — First edition.
pages    cm — (Studies on ethnic groups in China)
Includes bibliographical references and index.
ISBN 978-0-295-99306-5 (cloth : alk. paper); 978-0-295-99307-2 (pbk. : alk. paper)
1. Ethnology—China—Ganzi Zangzu Zizhizhou   2. Ethnicity—China—Ganzi Zangzu Zizhizhou   3. Matriarchy—China—Ganzi Zangzu Zizhizhou
4. Matrilineal kinship—China—Ganzi Zangzu Zizhizhou
5. Ganzi Zangzu Zizhizhou (China)—Ethnic relations.
6. Ganzi Zangzu Zizhizhou (China)—Social life and customs.   I. Title.
GN635.C5T46 2014
305.800951—dc23       2013018070

To Fredrik Barth, the kind of person I want to become.
Also to Robert Weller, a genuine mentor who has never given up on me.

# CONTENTS

CHAPTER 5

*The Moluo Tourism Association: How Far to Go?* 97

CONCLUSION 117

# FOREWORD

There are many Tibets. There is the administrative Tibet Autonomous Region, a province of the People's Republic of China. There is the geopolitical Tibet of the Government in Exile and its overseas supporters. There is the linguistic, religious, and cultural Tibet spread out over five provinces of China as well as parts of neighboring countries and diaspora communities. And there is the ideational Tibet of a venerable Buddhist civilization threatened by Chinese policies and globalization. But there is also the local Tibet of thousands of villages and townships, each with its own linguistic, sectarian, and cultural identity, and each with a different relationship to the Chinese regime and the global community. Suopo Township in Danba County, Sichuan, is one piece of this local Tibet, and Tenzin Jinba's *In the Land of the Eastern Queendom* tells a compelling story of how this piece of the local Tibet is being transformed by China's current tourism boom.

Danba is an area that is marginal in many respects. Marginal to China because it is sparsely populated and most of its inhabitants are ethnic Tibetans. Marginal to Tibet because it is part of the traditional eastern Tibetan province of Kham, outside the area previously administered by the Dalai Lama's government in Lhasa, with its own language and martial tradition. Marginal to Kham because most of its inhabitants speak various

Gyarong languages only distantly related to the Kham variety of Tibetan. And marginal to Gyarong because most of Gyarong is in a different prefecture. But despite its quadruple marginality, Danba in recent years has come firmly within the orbit of the ethnic and scenic tourism that has become a favorite pastime of the Chinese urban middle class. The local elites in many parts of Danba, including Suopo, have jumped to take advantage of the tourism boom, both for its possible monetary benefits and in order to promote and display local cultural heritage and encourage local pride in the area's culture and history.

As part of Danba's and Suopo's tourism boom, a dispute has recently arisen over the location of a legendary capital of the "Eastern Queendom" of the title, a matriarchal polity that may have existed a thousand years ago, as mentioned in Chinese historiographical literature. The book describes in lively detail the politics of the dispute, which involves ordinary villagers, community elites, and cadres serving at different levels of the state. Dr. Tenzin's insider-outsider position as a Gyarong native, as well as his U.S. PhD degree, give him a combination of insider access and outsider distance that enables him to describe these disputes in a way that contributes much to our knowledge of the politics of ethnicity and tourism not only in Tibet but in China more generally.

Why should we care about the Eastern Queendom, since it may or may not have ever existed? There are three good reasons. First, we need a more realistic and complex knowledge of Tibet. In an era when monks are self-immolating, governments are being repressive, and journalists are feasting on the more sensational aspects of that country's tragic recent history, more complex and subtle things are going on. Tibet is not uniform, and its relations with China are not fully adversarial, though of course almost all Tibetans long to see the authorities pursue more benevolent and less paranoid policies. This book helps to discredit any simplistic or romantic notions of Tibet. Second, we need to know more about ethnic tourism and local politics in China. As hundreds of millions of Chinese visit exotic places and peoples annually (and at least hundreds of thousands come to Danba), tourism not only affects local communities but also affects the way China is put together and the way people conceive of its being put together. Third and perhaps most importantly, we need more ethnographies of Tibetan communities. There are very few, and only a minority of these are based on intensive, long-term research by scholars like Dr. Tenzin who know the communities from the inside out and also have the academic tools to analyze their local politics and culture in sophisticated ways.

Read *In the Land of the Eastern Queendom* for its analytical insights and its descriptive richness, to be sure, but also read it for a great story, about modernization, development, tourism, politics, and intrigue amidst both spectacular natural scenery and complicated ethnic relations. We are proud to introduce the Eastern Queendom in this, volume 15 of Studies on Ethnic Groups in China.

STEVAN HARRELL

March 2013

# PREFACE AND ACKNOWLEDGMENTS

This book is about a small number of villagers at the far eastern edge of the Qinghai-Tibetan Plateau who are struggling to find a proper niche in the sociopolitical constitution of their native county, among the Gyarongwa and Tibetans, and in China. It is expected to build dialogue with two categories of queries from critical reviewers and potential readers: the scope of investigation and the issue of ethnicity. To be more specific, can this case study speak to a much broader range of issues regarding sociopolitical changes and state-society relations in Tibet and China beyond this seemingly trivial incident in a tiny, out-of-the-way place? Does ethnicity or Tibetanness matter in this case and also in this work?

This book displays the convergence of my general concerns and academic interests: Chinese nationalism and ethnic representations, civil association and social change, Chinese reform and collective action, tourism and modernity, the Tibetan riots of 2008 and their repercussions, border/ frontier and marginality, gender politics, ethnic (Tibetan) policy, grassroots (subaltern) agency, and so on. Simultaneously, it aims to bring to light the intricate and complex terrain in which the queendom dispute is situated. I also want to show that this case is both microscopic and panoramic, meaning that it deals with a local Tibetan society's transition as much as it addresses the transformation of Tibetan and Chinese societies in general. Likewise, it is as much about a borderland society as it is about the societies in the Chinese and Tibetan heartlands. Moreover, I expect some critiques of its "inadequate" attention to the locals' ethnicity, namely, the locals seem not to be ethnic or Tibetan enough. As a matter of fact, this is what I am striving for. Many of the works on ethnic groups in China tend to highlight their ethnic performativity—for instance, Tibetans do what Tibetans are supposed to do—but I want to show that ethnicity is just one of the multiple identities of the locals and doesn't matter to them all the time, even though it does play a role in the queendom dispute and their political agendas.The natives have the same problems as millions of other villagers or peasants throughout China, as they are all subject to Party-state policy and reform and to modernity and globalization with Chinese characteristics. However, I hope I have succeeded in balancing the difference and sameness, particularity and universality, regarding the locals' responses to social transformation vis-à-vis those of other Tibetan communities, the Han, and other minority villagers.

This book has been inspired by three major streams of influence: my own status as a Gyarong/Tibetan native, Victor Turner's idea of liminality, and James Scott's works on subordinate groups' resistance strategies, especially those occurring in borderlands like Zomia. Tsanlha Ngawang—a reincarnate lama and distinguished scholar on Gyarong—has been hoping that we could work together to dispel doubts about Gyarong's "authentic" Tibetan status. This was the plan for my PhD program in the United States, but it turns out that I have been fully "brainwashed" by sophisticated anthropological theories of ethnicity and identity; that is, instead of authenticating Gyarong's Tibetanness, I have been fascinated with the issue of how and why Gyarong's Tibetan identity becomes problematic. Turner's insights, added to Arnold van Gennep's writing on rites of passage, kindled my initial interest in the concept of liminality—a state of being "between and betwixt"—and this eventually fueled my visualization of borders as liminal spaces that are ruled by ambivalence, uncertainty, outsideness, namelessness, instability, resistance, temporariness, convertibility, and innovativeness. I have also benefited from Scott's approach to subordinate and borderland (e.g., Zomia) populations by spotlighting their agency in making the best out of disadvantages.

These inspirations, however, are inseparable from the training I received at the Anthropology Department of Boston University, which played an essential role in fostering my intellectual perspicacity and critical perspectives. Fredrik Barth has been the greatest influence on my life and career. He is the only person I have met so far in my life who can be described as both truly charismatic and decently humble. He showed me with his manners, dignity, and wisdom that a great scholar must be a great person in the first place. This book reflects my contemplation on his conceptualization of ethnic and cultural categories as unbounded entities interfacing with each other, as well as his advocacy of the significance of individual concerns, interests, positionality, and creativity in cultural analysis. Charles Lindholm enlightened my path with his scholarly sophistication and interdisciplinary approach, which helped shape the major themes in this book, for example, modernity, tourism, authenticity, and identity. Kimberly Arkin never tired of telling me that I could do better, and this book has been accomplished with her stimulation and urging. My encounter with Robert Weller, my chief adviser, was one of the greatest things that has ever happened in my life. I am inclined to count it a miracle, since he managed to turn such a naive and misplaced initiate into a "complicated" anthropologist. Therefore, this book is my most special gift for this exceptional mentor.

What I acquired from people with whom I worked in the field, who welcomed me with warmth and frankness, was no less than the contributions of the above-mentioned erudite scholars. Among them, I am most indebted to Uncle Tenzin. It was he who ushered me into the convoluted landscape of the queendom dispute and introduced me to his family, Moluo Tourism Association members, and other key informants in Suopo. All of them are either anonymous or pseudonymous in the book, but I hope they can feel my wholehearted appreciation for sharing their thoughts and concerns with me. At the same time, I am sorry if I have let them down by being unable to prove that the Eastern Queendom is theirs as they have hoped it would be.

A better book has been made possible with important feedback from the following scholars: Stevan Harrell, Emily Yeh, Lorri Hagman, Leonardo Schiocchet, Janet Gyatso, Merry White, John G. Blair, and Jerusha McCormack, to name just a few. So many others have also helped me in one way or another in the course of gathering ideas and completing this book, and I would love to extend my sincere thanks to Robert Hefner, Parker Shipton, Frank Korom, Jenny White, Charlene Makley, Gray Tuttle, Nicolas Sihlé, Navid Fozi-Abivard, Mentor Mustafa, Andrew Armstrong, Shelby Carpenter,

Naoko Nakagawa, Chelsea Shields Strayer, Sarah Tobin, Susan Costello, Chrystal Whelan, Ahmet Selim Tekelioglu, Mark Palmer, Kathy Kwasnica, Jiangye, and many more.

This book would not have been possible without the general support of the Cora Du Bois Charitable Trust, which granted me a dissertation writing fellowship, and the Fundamental Research Funds for the Central Universities from Lanzhou University (Project Title: The Reconfiguration of Grassroots Politics in Tibetan Regions in the Transitional Era with granting No: 12LZUJBWZD008).

Finally, I am grateful to the Agrarian Studies Program of Yale University for hosting me as a postdoctoral associate in 2013–14. This gives me the opportunity to make the best use of the university's dynamic and creative academic environment. Here I am able to continue my investigation of theoretical debates on borders/frontiers and marginality, collective resistance and political change, and grassroots associations and state-society relations as well as to amplify and extend my analytical model of convergence zone and strategic (or voluntary) marginality into the Himalayan region and Southeast Asia. Readers of this book will also see my further reflections on the issues discussed here and those that will be broadened and freshly explored in the near future. Thus I would like to thank all of you in advance for your continuing interest.

MAP 1. Gyarong (Rgyal rong), which spans portions of Kham, Amdo, and Sichuan. Adapted from Kolas and Thowsen 2005

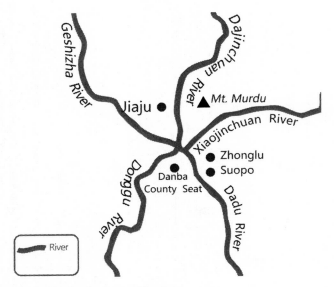

MAP 2. Danba County, major sites

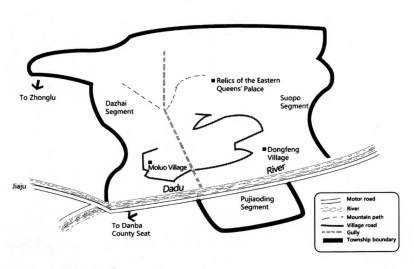

MAP 3. Suopo, sites of interest

In the Land of the Eastern Queendom

# INTRODUCTION

✳

In May 2005, an article in a local newspaper, "The Capital of the Eastern Queendom Comes to Light," rocked Danba County, Ganzi Tibetan Autonomous Prefecture, in Sichuan, China. The author, Uncle Pema—a cadre from Suopo Township in Danba—claimed that the capital of this legendary matriarchal kingdom was located precisely in Suopo. Key officials at both the prefectural and county levels were shocked and wasted no time in ordering an investigation into this matter. The reason for their uneasiness was that Danba County had already bestowed the title "Ancient Capital of the Eastern Queendom" (Dongnü Gudu) on Suopo's neighboring rival township, Zhonglu. So the article was seen as a direct challenge to county authorities. This incident marked a milestone in the efforts of Suopo elites and villagers to reclaim the queendom label. The Suopowa, or people from Suopo (wa means "people" in Tibetan), accused county officials of favoritism and partisanship. In pressing their claims, the Suopowa were seeking to take advantage of the media and initiate collective actions such as demonstrations and pleas to higher authority as well as make use of the legal space of their newly founded quasi-civil association, the Moluo Tourism Association (Moluo Lüyou Xiehui). However, the Suopowa's queendom discourse is full of puzzles and paradoxes that are key to our understanding of the nuances, complexity, and multidimensionality of the queendom dispute. It illuminates local Tibetans' concerns and interests, as their society is deeply entangled in unprecedented social transformation and engages more intensively with different levels of the state in response to China's all-inclusive political rearrangements and the ensuing consequences, exemplified by the unfolding intricacy of state-and-society interactions and the proliferation of collective actions throughout China.

The Suopowa's claim to a lineage connection with the matriarchal queens seems to contradict the pronouncement of their Tibetanness and their desire to identify with the Khampa—a Tibetan subgroup celebrated for its masculine culture. If the Suopowa take pride in their Tibetan identity, why do they label themselves as descendants of non-Tibetan queens? If the Suopowa advertise local males as authentic Khampa men, who are known for being well built, fiercely courageous, and socially unconstrained, why do they sell an apparently feminized image of themselves by declaring that women are more capable and politically sophisticated than men in Suopo? Then, if Suopo women are superior to men, why do they seem not to have played a more active role in the queendom struggle and other collective actions?

The Suopowa's political stance toward the state and the Chinese Communist Party is also full of puzzles: Why do most Suopowa speak highly of central state policy and the Party while Tibetans as a group are further marginalized in China's social and political structure as a result of the 2008 Tibetan riots? Why do they fiercely attack the local state for all the wrongs it has done to them while proclaiming their faith in the absolute justice and purity of the central state?

The queendom dispute occurs as Danba has become a nationally acclaimed tourist destination in China and as Danba people are increasingly aware of sexualized representations of local women in the tourist market. This period has also seen exacerbated conflicts within and among villages and townships as well as burgeoning antagonism and resistance against the local state—the county and township. These disputes, however, have little to do with the Tibetan desire for independence. The queendom dispute is not merely an accident or a product of broader Tibetan ethnic politics; instead, it stems from the marginalized status of local people in both Tibetan and Chinese societies and also their experience of modernizing economic and social change in a distinctive local setting. Therefore, the Suopowa's local political pursuit must also be located within a macroscopic picture of transformations in Chinese society. Thus, the Suopowa's queendom struggle is simultaneously unique because it is embedded in particular ethnic, cultural, social, and political contexts and not unique because it is a reflection of the profound repercussions and implications of China's reforms and social change, as showcased in intensified contention between state and society and the boom in various kinds of intermediate associations all over China.

The Suopowa's perception of marginality, both real and imagined, informs their negotiations of multiple identities and their modernist pursuit of a better life, culturally, economically, and politically. Their marginalized status among both the Han and Tibetans as well as their assumed political peripherality in Danba County are conducive to their reconfigurations of ethnic, political, regional, and other identities. The Suopowa utilize their marginality either as a means of subverting their peripheral position or for the sake of anticipated political goals. In this way, the attribution of marginality sets the stage for their constant negotiations and orchestration of their multiple identities—on the one hand, they have to conform to the framework prescribed by the state and pursue their political aspirations in accordance with that framework, but on the other hand, they are left with much room for playing with and maneuvering within this framework.

As members of a minority ethnic group, and especially as members of the officially identified Zangzu (Tibetan ethnic group), the Suopowa are subject to China's ethnic and Zangzu policies. Despite the state's efforts to incorporate Zangzu as an integral part of China, their cultural and linguistic differences and, particularly, the supposedly rebellious nature of some Zangzu distinguish them from the Han and most other less different and thus "loyal" and "patriotic" minorities. Therefore, the Suopowa's queendom struggle and political claims are informed by this broad social and political environment that has placed them on the margin. As "colorful" and "exotic" minority members, the Suopowa's identities and self-representations are shaped and structured by the official/state and Han popular discourses. Their queendom and other political claims as well as their identity quests are embedded in their marginalized position among Zangzu. The Suopowa and the Gyarongwa (people of Gyarong) as a whole—a subgroup to which the Suopowa belong—are situated on the periphery of the Tibetan ethnic group and are often not recognized as "authentic" Tibetans in the eyes of many "mainstream" Tibetans. The Suopowa's contested Tibetan identity has had a profound impact on their identity construction and political positioning. Simultaneously, their struggle for the queendom label also derives from their perceived or imagined political peripherality in Danba—that is, they complain that they have been neglected and taken for granted by the county government. The queendom dispute serves only as an outlet for the expression of such a status on the sociopolitical map of Danba County. Therefore, their queendom discourse is a direct response to and reflection of their ethnic and political marginalities and plays out in the framework of these marginalities.

Yet marginality should not be looked at as merely a constraint that circumscribes actors' choices. Marginality can also be an opportunity to act as agents. Marginality connotes difference, uniqueness, and, therefore, authenticity in certain circumstances. The Suopowa appropriate their ethnic marginality in order to construct an image of their distinctiveness among all Zangzu subgroups and, thus, their irreplaceable role and "authentic" status in the Tibetan family. They also use this marginality to advertise Suopo as an exceptional and particularly appealing destination in the Chinese tourism market. Making use of their political marginality, the Suopowa hope for possible compensation or rewards from the state and also outsiders' attention to their grievances and political claims. In so doing, they sometimes situate themselves on the margins, as they consider a state of strategic marginality to be instrumental in engendering positive changes and achieving anticipated political goals.

## THE SINO-TIBETAN BORDER AS A CONVERGENCE ZONE

The Suopowa's identity construction is inseparable from their multiple marginalities as well as the constraints and opportunities these may evoke, and this state of being has everything to do with their status as a people on the Sino-Tibetan border. Therefore, it is necessary to reexamine the concept of border to see how the redefined border illustrates the fluidity and elasticity of marginality and helps identify and unravel the convoluted intricacy of the queendom discourse.

The concept of a border or frontier embodies marginality or peripherality—a state of being distant or withdrawn from sociopolitical and cultural centers or mainstreams; thus the border often becomes a site of escape and flight from the state or similarly powerful political entities (Scott 2009).

Many scholars have pointed out that borderlands are also sites of heterogeneity and transcultural dialogue (Tsing 1993), "interstitial zones" (Gupta 1992)—creative grounds for the making and unmaking of often competing sociocultural worlds (Makley 2003, 598)—or sites for "(border) crossing" (Rosaldo 1993) and transgressing boundaries (Ewing 1998) that entail creative cultural productions and intersections of power and difference.[1] Therefore, borders are locations not simply where political or cultural territories end but where they meet, contest, negotiate, converge, and fuse and thus where hybrid and new cultures and identities flourish.

Danba, part of the Gyarong region, is situated on the border of the Han and Tibetan regions both geographically and culturally. Danba and Gyarong exemplify the ambiguity, mobility, vitality, creativity, restlessness, and diversity of the border. Thus, Danba and Gyarong may be seen not as peripheral to both the Han and Tibetans but as a convergence zone where the Han and Tibetan peoples and cultures connect, interact, exchange, compete, blend, and coexist. They are places where locals not only incorporate various elements from these two peoples and cultures but also carve out a new space for their survival, cultural expressions, identity construction, and political positioning. The term "convergence zone" may embrace hybridity (Bhabha 1994) and creolization (Hannerz 1992); however, this notion best describes Gyarong's in-between status as well as its distinctiveness in relation to the Han and Tibetans.

A hybridized condition requires a space where the center and the periphery (e.g., colonizers and the colonized, or the West and the East) are no longer positioned as antitheses but exist in dialectic ongoing interactions with "intertwined histories and engagement across dichotomies" (Prakash 1994, 1486; see Bhabha 1994). As a consequence, the hybrid breaks down the symmetry and duality of self/other, inside/outside (Bhabha 1994, 165). In this way, hybridity opens up a space of ambivalence and ambiguity characterized by the blurring of the once clear-cut center-periphery boundary. Thus it creates a possibility for the once marginalized to move from the periphery toward the center. Nevertheless, the center will simultaneously remap itself as the authority and embodiment of purity and authenticity in contrast to the peripheral "bastards" who are very close to "us/white" but not quite "white," or who simply present black skins with white masks (ibid., 88, 172; see also Fanon 2008).

The idea of creolization demonstrates a similar form of interaction between the center and the periphery. Creolized cultures are seen to be saturated with power structure and asymmetric relations because the cultures that interact are not equal to each other and at least one is always situated in a dominant position; however, the cultural processes of creolization involve much more creative center-periphery interactions (Hannerz 1992). A new (creolized) culture emerges out of multidimensional cultural encounters as unique combinations and creations.[2] Therefore, creolized cultures are not simple replicas of dominant cultures; instead, they are combinations of innovative and selective appropriations of dominant cultural forms and indigenous readings and applications of them in a particular local context. The agency of the marginal is underscored in the way that the periphery is believed not only to be able to talk back but also to possess the potential of rising as the center (ibid., 266).

The notions of hybridity and creolization are useful for identifying aspects of a dynamic convergence zone. Gyarong forms a hybridized or creolized society due to the considerable impacts of the Han/state and Tibetans on local cultures, politics, and identities in their intensive encounters. Gyarong's representations and positioning vis-à-vis the Han/state and Tibetans exemplify the dialectic interplay between the center and the periphery as illustrated by these notions. A noteworthy example is the locals' use of their ambivalent ethnic and linguistic origins and their marginal status as leverage in negotiating their identities with the centers. Nevertheless, both concepts still tend to underline the predominant role and "purity" of the center and thus the secondary value of the periphery. As a result, the relatively separate cultural forms and distinctive identities of peripheral societies are left unattended.

What distinguishes the idea of a convergence zone from these two notions is the importance it attaches to a peripheral society's status as an active local center. As a convergence zone, Gyarong is the site where the Han and Tibetan centers coalesce, fuse, and contend and where the local society engages and intersects with the Han and Tibetan centers simultaneously. In this instance, Gyarong is not always in a peripheral position; in fact, in local discourse, Gyarong is viewed as a dynamic center. What comes out of these multiple encounters and convergences is a new, heterogeneous, and dynamic Gyarong culture and identity. This new culture and identity carry imprints from both of the centers, but in this convergence zone, one also sees the flourishing of distinctive local culture and identity. Therefore, Gyarong society is not simply the equivalent of Tibetan elements plus Han/state components. Gyarong society has its own indigenous traditions and local sociopolitical contexts; thus, Gyarong stands as a relatively independent political and cultural entity. This suggests that the Suopowa's queendom struggle and identity construction are embedded not only in engagement and contention between state politics and Tibetan identity/ethno-nationalism but also in the local society's distinctive historical, cultural, and political contexts and its positioning vis-à-vis the Han/state and Tibetans.

The queendom discourse is deconstructed not so much through the marginalizing of the Gyarongwa and the Suopowa as through their persistent efforts to challenge or even reverse the dominant discourse and political structure that often place them at a disadvantage. Their ingenious application of their peripheral status, noteworthy strategic marginality, is rooted in their liminal standing as a people straddling two worlds on the Sino-Tibetan border—a convergence zone where a dynamic center-periphery paradigm is constantly reconfigured and renegotiated. They are peripheral to the Han/state center and the Tibetan center but are simultaneously ushered into both; alternatively, they take the initiative and validate their unequivocal centrality, and in their local representations, Gyarong is also seen as a self-sustained vital center. In this way, three major dimensions of their identity are brought into being: worthy Chinese citizens, "authentic" Tibetans, and distinctive Gyarongwa. Each of these identities and other derivative identities come to prominence in different contexts. Although the Suopowa cannot always choose who or what they are, they have managed to secure space for manipulating these and other identities to their advantage. In constructing and negotiating their identities, they activate and invigorate an intertwined network of sociopolitical restructurings: evolving Chinese ethnic landscape and fluctuating Tibetan policy, the repositioning of the local society vis-à-vis the township, county, and other levels of the state, and an upsurge in collective action or rural unrest as well as the heterogenization of the societal sector and the state. This state of being will not only bring to light the nuanced and involuted sociopolitical landscape of the queendom discourse but also provide a glimpse into transforming Chinese, Tibetan, and Gyarong societies.

Chapter 1

SETTING FOOT IN THE QUEEN'S LAND

*

The Suopowa's queendom discourse is not simply a product of tourism propaganda, nor is the uncovering of the Eastern Queendom (Dongnüguo) merely an accident. Occurring at a time of sweeping social and political changes, this discourse sheds light on the Suopowa's negotiation of various identities and their initiatives for strategizing marginality in pursuit of their political objectives. The Suopowa's peripheral status vis-à-vis the Han/state, and Tibetans has been critical in shaping this discourse, and their struggle exemplifies China's ethnic policy and Tibetan politics. How did the Suopowa and the Gyarongwa become "official Tibetans," or Zangzu, in the first place? And how does their contested Tibetan identity inform their choices and concerns through the queendom dispute? Was the queendom discovery coincidental? Under what circumstances was the queendom unearthed? And how has the queendom discourse been propagated?

MAPPING THE EASTERN QUEENDOM

Scholars point out that the title "Eastern Queendom" was used to describe two different political entities at the time of the Sui (581–618) and Tang (618–

907) dynasties: one south of Cong Ling, or the Pamir Mountains (running across western China and southeastern Central Asia), or, more precisely, in western Tibet adjacent to the Himalayas (Shi 2009a), and the other somewhere between Tibet and Sichuan.[1] The exact location of the second differs in Chinese historical sources: the *Book of Sui* (Suishu) and the *History of Northern Dynasties* (Beishi) suggest it was in today's Chamdo (C: Changdu) in the east of the present-day Tibet Autonomous Region, while the *Old Tang History* (Jiu Tangshu) and the *New Tang History* (Xin Tangshu) indicate that it was in the Dajinchuan region (today's Jinchuan and Danba Counties) in western Sichuan.[2] Most scholars tend to favor one over the other, and thus no consensus has been reached. According to Guo Shengbo (2002), there are two other plausible explanations that have often been overlooked: first, that there were two Eastern Queendoms located somewhere between Tibet and Sichuan and, second, that the queendom in Chamdo migrated to the Dajin-chuan region in western Sichuan. Guo espouses the second claim, arguing that the migration occurred in the first half of the seventh century when the rising Tibetan empire severely threatened the Chamdo queendom's survival or invaded its territory.

Many scholars acknowledge that the record of the Eastern Queendom in the *Old Tang History* is more accurate than the record in the *New Tang History*, which conflates the queendom in western Tibet and the one in western Sichuan. Nevertheless, some accounts of the Eastern Queendom in western Tibet in the *Book of Sui* are almost exactly the same as those of the Eastern Queendom in western Sichuan in the *Old Tang History*, such as the use of ornithomancy—divination by the use of birds—burial practices for nobles, the reign of a major and a lesser queen, succession practices, and housing styles. Some scholars argue that these two queendoms did have much in common, yet others assert that the queendom in western Tibet migrated to western Sichuan. According to Shi Shuo, it would have been nearly impossible for these two queendoms to share so many similarities considering the distance between them, diverse geographic and ecological environments, and different modes of livelihood; in addition, a move to western Sichuan would not have been practical (see Shi 2009a). Thus, Shi argues that the *Old Tang History* incorporates accounts of the queendom in western Tibet from the *Book of Sui* in its depiction of the queendom in western Sichuan. In his view, the name "Eastern Queendom" originally referred exclusively to the one in western Tibet and was also used for the one in western Sichuan at the turn of the ninth century. Therefore, the existence of one single title in documenting two different Eastern Queendoms in historical works has resulted in confusion for later historians and modern-day scholars. He concluded that the records of queendom customs and political systems such as ornithomancy, burial traditions, ruling and succession practices, and housing styles were incompatible with those of the queendom in western Sichuan and thus were historical accounts of the queendom in western Tibet instead.

Although there has been wider acknowledgment among scholars today that the Eastern Queendom was located in the Jinchuan region in western Sichuan, many have overlooked the distinction identified by Shi Shuo. Therefore, scholars commonly use various unfiltered accounts of different queendoms from the *Book of Sui*, the *New Tang History*, the *Old Tang History*, or other historical canons in describing the ancient practices of this specific queendom in western Sichuan. Some also identify these features among today's Gyarongwa residing in the Jinchuan region, who are believed to descend from the ancient queens and their subjects. In this way, an equation between Gyarong and the Eastern Queendom is roughly established.

Queendom traditions allegedly evident among the Gyarongwa include housing styles, women's clothing, an abundance of beautiful women, women's high status, and courtship and marriage customs; these are offered as proof of the "uninterrupted" heritage passed down from the ancient Eastern Queendom.[3] According to the *Old Tang History* and other historical records, the queen lived in a nine-story building, while commoners lived in six-story houses. Some scholars equate these structures with the stone watchtowers (C: *diaolou*) that were and are still spread all over Gyarong (Wang Huailin 2006). Gyarong women wear a long cloak over their shoulders and a special kind of skirt with dozens of pleats or folds, both of which are said to have been inherited from the queens, and their beauty is claimed as proof that they carry the noble blood of elegant queens.

In the queendom, women supposedly had absolute control in the socio-political sphere and held official posts, leaving men with lowly positions such as aides and soldiers. Correspondingly, Gyarong women are said to enjoy high status at home and in society. Some authors interpret various queendom practices documented in historical works, such as polyandry (one woman with multiple husbands) and matrilineal kinship (children carrying on the lineage of the maternal line), as a sign of romance and free love. These scholars claim that Gyarong courtship and marriage customs such as "climbing the wall," in which a young man climbs the wall and sneaks into his lover's room at night, are equally "romantic" (Ma 2006; Wang Huailin 2006). Some also point out that the name of Gyarong and the names of other geographic features, such as the Dadu River, are unambiguously connected with the queendom (Ma Chengfu 2006; Wang Huailin 2006). In Tibetan, the full name of Gyarong and of the Dadu River start with "Rgyal Mo" (The Queen), suggesting that there was a queen who used to rule Gyarong, and thus Gyarong is the Land of Women, as is the Eastern Queendom.

Various scholars highlight these cultural and historical connections between Gyarong and the Eastern Queendom in order to justify their claims that the queendom used to exist in today's Gyarong, although the exact location of the queendom or its capital is in dispute. Some claim that it was situated in Jinchuan County, Aba Tibetan and Qiang Autonomous Prefecture (Aba Zangzu Qiangzu Zizhizhou), while others contend that it was in Danba County, Ganzi Tibetan Autonomous Prefecture (Ganzi Zangzu Zizhizhou). Proponents for each location are predominantly scholars, cadres, or officials originally from or working in that particular area. Both counties take advantage of media and scholarship to promote their claims. However, due to Danba's influence in the tourist market, as well as its association with the Valley of Beauties, its claim has received more attention. Nevertheless, even within Danba, two townships, Suopo and Zhonglu, compete for the queendom.

## DEFINING THE FIELD SETTING

Danba County (30°23'–31°29' N, 101°17'–102°13' E) is under the jurisdiction of Ganzi Tibetan Autonomous Prefecture in western Sichuan, in southwestern China. It is an important eastern entrance to Ganzi prefecture from the Chengdu Plain. Its altitude ranges from 1,700 to 5,820 meters (5,577–19,094 feet). The county seat is 1,842 meters (6,043 feet) above sea level. The summit of Mount Murdu, the most important holy mountain in the Gyarong region, which lies within the territory of Danba, is at 4,820 meters (15,813 feet). Five major rivers run through Danba, of which the Dadu River is the biggest.

Danba administers fifteen townships and 181 villages with an area of 5,649 square kilometers (2,181 square miles). It has a population of a little over sixty thousand. Zangzu make up 77 percent of the total population. The Han, Qiang, Hui, and other minority ethnic groups compose the rest of the population. In Danba, Zangzu residents speak four major languages or dialects. Roughly 37 percent of the total Zangzu population in Danba speak a Kham Tibetan dialect, about 34 percent speak the Ergong language/dialect, nearly 27 percent speak the Gyarong "official" language/dialect, and the remaining 2 percent speak the nomadic Amdo Tibetan dialect (Lin Junhua 2006b). Each language/dialect is incomprehensible to speakers of the others. As a result, Chinese, specifically the Sichuan dialect, has become the standard language of communication among various Zangzu groups in Danba.

Danba's economy was based largely on logging and agriculture until 1998, when China launched the large-scale Natural Forest Resources Preservation Project (Tianranlin Ziyuan Baohu Gongcheng), which aimed to protect the environment in the upper and middle reaches of the Yangzi River and the Yellow River. Due to the breathtaking landscape, magnificent stone watchtowers, and exquisite Tibetan-style farmers' houses as well as the area's reputation for an abundance of beautiful women, the Chinese tourist market has held Danba in increasing esteem since 2000, and tourism has become one of the pillars of Danba's economy.

The seat of Suopo Township is merely 5 kilometers (3.1 miles) away from the county seat. This township has an area of 138.8 square kilometers (53.6 square miles). It is composed of eleven administrative villages with 664 households and 3,333 residents. The Han make up a little more than 6 percent of the whole population, and most of them are from Dongfeng Village; Zangzu villagers normally refer to them as the Han Gang (Hantuan). Zangzu villagers in Suopo speak a Khampa dialect, but most men and the majority of women under the age of fifty can speak either fluent or comprehensible Sichuan dialect. The Dadu River cuts across the township, and Moluo Village, where the township government is located and also where I did most of my fieldwork, is situated on the eastern bank of this river. It has sixty-three households with a population of 232, of which only two are Han. Suopo is well known for its large number of stone watchtowers, and Moluo, with its cluster of imposing and spectacular watchtowers of different styles—quadrangular, pentagonal, octagonal (see fig. 1.1)—has been designated a Famous Historical and Cultural Village of China (Zhongguo Lishi

FIG. 1.1. Ancient watchtowers of Moluo, Suopo, along the Dadu River, 2009.
Photo by the author

Wenhua Mingcun) by the Ministry of Housing and Urban-Rural Development and the State Administration of Cultural Heritage.

Danba, including Suopo, is part of the Gyarong region, which is situated
on the southeastern fringe of the Qinghai-Tibetan Plateau.[4] Most parts of
Gyarong are included in today's Aba Tibetan and Qiang Autonomous Prefecture in Sichuan, while Danba belongs administratively to Ganzi Tibetan
Autonomous Prefecture.[5] Gyarong as a whole covers an area of roughly
160,000 square kilometers (61,776 square miles); it is more than four times
as big as Taiwan (Quedan 1995). This region used to be ruled by officially
recognized *tusi,* local chiefs, or the kings.[6] Gyarong is popularly referred
to as the Eighteen Kingdoms of Gyarong (T: Rgyal Rong Rgyal Khab Bco
Brgyad). The Gyarong region is inhabited not only by the Gyarongwa but
also by Tibetans from two other Tibetan subgroups—Amdo Tibetans and
Khampa Tibetans—as well as ethnic Qiang, Han, Hui, and others. The
overall number of the Gyarongwa is about 300,000.[7] Gyarong has several

distinct languages/dialects, and linguists are still debating their classification. Despite such linguistic differences, generally speaking, speakers of various dialects recognize each other as Gyarongwa.

## INSIDER FROM THE OUTSIDE
## AND OUTSIDER FROM THE INSIDE

I am a Gyarongwa, and my native tongue is the "official" language of Gyarong (Rgyal Rong skad). As a Gyarong local, I have been constantly questioned by other Tibetans about my own and the Gyarongwa's Tibetan identity. Consequently, along with other Gyarongwa, especially intellectuals, I am required to constantly negotiate both my Gyarong identity and my Tibetan identity. Thus, as an insider, I have empathy for the Suopowa's struggle for the queendom brand as well as their denial of Gyarongness. Due largely to my local connection, many Suopowa whom I encountered and interacted with believed that, as "one of them," I could understand their frustrations and concerns. Thus, I was able to witness various aspects of the locals' daily lives and hear about their frustrations, hopes, and desires during my one year of fieldwork in Suopo (June 2008–June 2009) and multiple short trips for fieldwork in 2007, 2010, 2011, and 2012. I also gained the trust of Uncle Pema, a Suopo township cadre and the principal queendom advocate, and members of the Moluo Tourism Association, who expected that as a scholar from Gyarong, I would undoubtedly play a part in preserving and promoting local cultural traditions, including queendom legends and customs. Thus, I was invited to participate in their meetings as their "cultural consultant" and offer my suggestions for the association's agendas and development programs. Likewise, due to my local roots, I had relatively easy access to more than forty township and county cadres and officials, most of whom talked freely about the nepotism, power struggles, and bureaucracy prevalent in Danba, cadre-peasant relations, and governmental agendas as well as discussed China's Tibetan and other policies.

I am also an outsider. My outsiderness matters not only in terms of how I was treated by locals but also in how I reflected upon my own position. Sometimes the Suopowa saw me as "one of them" because of my Gyarong background and local connections. Nevertheless, due to the difference between my native Gyarong tongue and their Khampa dialect—a sign of their "authentic" Tibetan origin—some people referred to me as "(one of) you Gyarongwa." Since I was from outside Suopo, I didn't have lineage and sociopolitical ties with them, either. Therefore, for many of them, I was merely a curious unrelated observer who would leave for good at a certain point. In my intensive interactions with the Suopowa, I came to realize how little that I, a Gyarong local, had known about them. This had much to do with my anthropological training in the United States. I have been exposed to different ideas and thoughts in books, lectures, and discussions as well as to the complexity and diversity of American society. I have also cultivated sensitivity toward things I had taken for granted; I now think twice about the "thick" meanings behind them. Being brought into direct contact with the concepts of ethnicity and other identities as "constructed," "imagined," and "invented" has revolutionized my mind. Such experiences have been instrumental in developing my new perspective toward Tibetan and Gyarong societies and identities. I started to drop the essentialist frame of mind that had inclined me to propagate Tibetan greatness and Gyarong distinctiveness and to see Tibetan and Gyarong identities as "naturally born" rather than socially constructed and politically informed. In this way, I have become an outsider to Tibetan and Gyarong societies.

When I looked at Suopo and Gyarong as an outsider, a completely new world opened up in front of me, as if I had never known the local society. What struck me most in the field were the Suopowa's global outlook and complexity. Many villagers I encountered did not hesitate to express their concerns about the queendom dispute, Suopo's marginalized status in Danba, the bureaucracy of the township and county government, village elections and factionalism, the prospects for tourism, the consequences of the Tibetan riots, the Beijing Olympic Games, China's international status, the United States' role in the world, and so on. Although they are often dismissed as narrow-minded "peasants" (*nongmin*), their knowledge of domestic and world affairs and of various policies in China showed me how complicated and modern the Suopowa really are. Their multifarious concerns also kept reminding me of what a labyrinthine web of connections the queendom dispute invokes. Thus, I became more and more aware that by looking at the queendom dispute merely as a village or regional matter, one runs the risk of losing sight of the complexity and intricacy of the whole picture.

## DISCOVERING THE EASTERN QUEENDOM

Few Danba locals had heard of the Eastern Queendom before 2004. The spread of the name "Eastern Queendom" has much to do with Mr. Wang, then head of the Propaganda Department of Ganzi prefecture. Mr. Wang is very interested in the Eastern Queendom's history and culture and has been writing about it since the early 2000s. He argues that the queendom did exist and that Danba still maintains many of its cultural traditions, such as the courtship and marriage customs, the architectural style of stone watchtowers, women's dress styles, religious beliefs (e.g., Bon, or Bon po, an indigenous Tibetan religion), life rituals such as the girls' puberty ritual, and so on (Wang Huailin 2006). He claims that some of these cultural elements can also be found now at Lugu Lake on the border of Sichuan and Yunnan—the well-known Women's Country (Nüerguo)—and some other places but that Danba was the hub of the queendom culture as well as its political center. At first he didn't specify the exact location of the palace of this queendom in Danba. Since he was one of the most important officials in Ganzi prefecture, his words had considerable weight among Danba officials. Danba County's Party committee and government started to collect evidence of the queendom's historical existence throughout the county. This task was carried out chiefly by two units: the Propaganda Department and the Culture and Tourism Bureau.

The county's action was not simply about taking orders from higher authorities but also had much to do with its ambitious project of advancing Danba's image in the Chinese tourist market. County officials were fully aware that the queendom label would be "exotic" and "mysterious" enough to attract the attention of tourists, so they ordered the appropriate department to search Danba for more substantial proof, such as relics, folk tales, and traditions, that would authenticate this claim. When the Culture and Tourism Bureau sent its instructions down to Suopo Township, the township head (*xiangzhang*) had no clue what the Eastern Queendom was but assigned the task of investigating it to his subordinate, Uncle Pema. Uncle Pema was regarded as the best person for this assignment because, as a Suopo native, he knew the local people and language and was keen on the study of local legends and history. However, according to him, he was completely at a loss when given this task because he had never heard of the Eastern Queendom. He started to think about writing something on local legends so that he would not be blamed for doing nothing, and in the process of collecting Suopo legends, he became convinced that there must be a connection between Suopo and the Eastern Queendom. In Suopo, stories about the queens were very popular with villagers. Local legend says that a queen from somewhere else fled to Suopo hundreds of years ago; she kept moving her residence until she found the ideal site for her palace on a cliff where the topography formed a natural barrier against invaders. The ruins of the palace still remain, and some locals were said to have seen an apparition of the queen and her retinue there before the 1980s. Since the queen was known as the "queen of (or from) the East" (*shar mo rje [?] rgyal po*), this coincides perfectly with the name of the Eastern Queendom. Uncle Pema was convinced that the legendary queens in Suopo must be the ones who had ruled the Eastern Queendom. Since then, he has become a devoted and energetic advocate of Suopo as the site of the queendom's palace.

Having made up his mind, he began to write out the queendom legends he had recorded. However, since he had only a primary school education, he thought it would be too hard to complete the task by himself. In May 2005, an old friend, the vice-head of Danba's Propaganda Department, who had worked in Suopo Township in the 1980s, came to inspect the township. After being ushered into Uncle Pema's home, he happened to see the draft. He was very excited about this great discovery but also concerned about its consequences. If what Uncle Pema recounted here was newly invented instead of being authentic legends, Uncle Pema and this official, who was in charge of the collection of queendom legends, would have serious problems, since the county government had already endorsed Zhonglu's claim to being the site of the queendom's ancient capital. Uncle Pema assured his friend that everything he had written was a truthful account of popular local legends that had been passed down since ancient times. Convinced of Uncle Pema's sincerity, this official promised that he would edit the manuscript and have it published by the local newspaper. The article was given the sensational title "The Capital of the Eastern Queendom Comes to Light" (*Dongnüguo guodu fuchu shuimian*). This article proved to be a great shock for some key officials at both the prefectural and county levels. The prefecture's Propaganda Department telephoned the head of Danba County's Propaganda Department several times on the same day, ordering the latter to investigate. The head of the Danba Propaganda Department was also summoned by the county's Party secretary to explain the situation, and Uncle Pema and his friend became the focus of attention. Uncle Pema was more than happy to see the commotion this article generated since it sent an important message to the county government that the queen's palace was located nowhere but in Suopo.

Uncle Pema's discovery put the county's leading officials in a delicate situation: they couldn't dismiss his assertion out of hand because Mr. Wang, who represented higher authorities, was impressed with the article and expressed his support for its claim after completing an investigative journey in December 2005; however, the county had already started to promote Zhonglu Township as the capital of the queendom. As a result, the Danba government decided to take a wait-and-see attitude. In my interviews with Uncle Pema, local elites, and villagers, most argued that the leadership's ambivalent attitude resulted from the fact that some important county officials were Zhonglu natives and were believed to be manipulating the queendom agenda. Uncle Pema and his supporters were upset about this "fact" and urged the county to deliver justice to Suopo by withholding its support for the Zhonglu clique. Suopo queendom advocates took advantage of the media and other opportunities to present their campaign to a wider public. Their claim was supported by more and more villagers, who pressured the county to reconsider its queendom agenda. As a consequence, the county government had to take the Suopowa's claim more seriously in order to prevent the Suopowa from taking radical actions against them. This explains why although Zhonglu Township was officially renamed Dongnügu Township (Township of the Eastern Women's Valley) in 2007, the change was never made public, and it is still known as Zhonglu Township.

Uncle Pema has played the most important role in promulgating Suopo's queendom discourse. He not only "discovered" the Eastern Queendom but also successfully engaged a large number of Suopo elites and villagers in the struggle for the queendom label that had been "stolen" by Zhonglu with the supposed complicity of county officials who were acting out of favoritism. Uncle Pema and his supporters contend that the Suopowa are "authentic" descendants of the ancient queens, that queendom traditions such as the girls' puberty ritual remain vital in local life, and that the queendom heritage is evident in Suopo women's status, which is higher than men's. A frequently cited example is that three female village heads of Suopo were sent to Beijing to meet with Chairman Mao Zedong in the 1950s and 1960s because of their exceptional leadership and extraordinary capacities, which were unmatched by men.

## BECOMING MARGINALIZED TIBETANS

Gyarong had relatively independent political entities, distinctive traditions, and a characteristic identity in relation to other Tibetans long before Liberation in 1950. However, the Chinese government's nationwide ethnic identification project has had profound impacts on the Gyarongwa's identity construction, as it has for all officially identified ethnic groups in China including the Han. The Gyarongwa's classification as Zangzu, or "official Tibetans," has evoked their Tibetan awareness, but that classification has contributed to their marginalized status within the Tibetan ethnic group. This situation underlies their struggle to find their proper niche among Tibetans and in China's ethnic and political landscape.

When China launched its ethnic identification project in 1950, the newly liberated Gyarongwa were first identified as Gyarongzu (*zu* means "ethnic group"). But because of persistent petitions and protests from former nobles who were recruited by the Party into the leadership in today's Aba Tibetan and Qiang Autonomous Prefecture in Sichuan, the Gyarongwa were officially recognized as Zangzu in 1954; however, the Gyarongwa's Tibetan identity has been questioned by other Tibetans and scholars ever since. The majority of Tibetans either deny the Gyarongwa's Zangzu status or proclaim the inadequacy of their Tibetanness. As a result, many Gyarongwa feel that they are marginalized, and some choose to identify with the Khampa, as the Suopowa and other Danba people tend to do. In extreme cases, they do not reveal their Gyarongness in their interactions with other Zangzu.[8] In reaction, some Gyarongwa emphasize their uniqueness and invaluable traditions in comparison to other Zangzu, a claim that has gathered momentum through the process of tourism development. Nevertheless, most Gyarongwa take pride in both their Zangzu status and their Gyarongness. This creates a dilemma for the Gyarongwa identity—they are Tibetans, at least officially, yet they are not Tibetan. This dilemma has informed their struggle to find their place in the Tibetan family as well as in China's ethnic and political terrain.

The controversy over the Gyarongwa's Tibetanness has to do first with the disputable place-name and group name Gyarong: Rgyal Rong or Rgya Rong. Most Tibetan scholars agree that "Rgyal Rong" is the correct spelling and accurate appellation from ancient Tibetan texts (Btsan Lha 1994; Dmu Dge 1997). "Rgyal Rong" is said to be an abbreviation of "Shar Rgyal Mo Tsa

Ba Rong," which means "the temperate agricultural area ruled by the queen in the east" or "the temperate agricultural area around Mount Murdu in the east." The slight difference between these two interpretations derives from the connotation of the expression "Rgyal Mo." Both groups of scholars agree that "Rgyal Mo" literally means "the queens," but the second version goes further by saying that "Rgyal Mo" is the short form of "Rgyal Mo Dmu Rdo"—the full name of Mount Murdu, the most sacred mountain in this region. However, another common interpretation identifies the name of Gyarong as Rgya Rong (Ma 1944). "Rgya" literally means "Han," so "Rgya Rong" means "the agricultural area close to the Han region."

The existence of these two divergent interpretations suggests the ambiguity of Gyarong's origin and history.[9] Therefore, deciphering the meaning of the term "Gyarong" is often regarded by scholars as a first essential step toward bringing Gyarong's history out of obscurity. As far as strong advocates for the spelling "Rgyal Rong" are concerned, relating the Gyarongwa to the Han is a serious misinterpretation of Gyarong's Tibetan origin. Rejecting the general claim that Gyarong was not Tibetanized until it was taken over and governed by the Tibetan empire from the seventh to ninth century, these advocates argued that Gyarong has been ethnically Tibetan since antiquity, as documented in Tibetan literature (Dmu Dge 1997; Btsan Lha 2007). However, a relatively mild reading of Gyarong's history and origin by other proponents for this spelling is that the Gyarongwa are a hybrid of different peoples who were later assimilated with the expansion of the Tibetan Empire. Therefore, they contend that the Gyarongwa descend not from a single line, namely, Tibetans, but from multiple sources as recorded in ancient Chinese literature: *Ranmang* in two Han periods (206 BCE–220 CE), *Jialiangyi* in the Sui dynasty (581–618), and *Xishan zhuqiang* (various Qiang peoples of Xishan) in the seventh and eighth centuries, as well as invading Tibetans in the seventh to ninth centuries.[10]

Although Tibetans most commonly refer to this region as Rgya Rong, "the agricultural area close to the Han region," their emphasis is often not on geographic proximity but on cultural and ethnic closeness to the Han. If the Gyarongwa are not so different from the Han, how can they qualify as Tibetans who have a distinctive language and unique cultural traditions? The legitimacy of the Gyarongwa's Tibetan identity is thus questioned.

The most noticeable difference between the Gyarongwa and other Zangzu is linguistic, and in most cases, the latter's doubt of Gyarong's Tibetanness is based on this easily perceived distinction. People from other Zangzu regions and the Gyarongwa themselves argue that the Gyarongwa speak a totally different language that has little similarity to "standard Tibetan." Although native speakers of one of the three primary Tibetan dialects from three major Tibetan subregions—Central Tibet (Ü-Tsang), Amdo, and Kham—cannot necessarily communicate with one another very easily, linguistic variations among these dialects are largely perceived as differences within a single language.

What other Zangzu refer to as "Gyarong language" is, in fact, only one of several languages/dialects spoken in the Gyarong region, although it is the principal one in Gyarong and is spoken by the largest population. It is often labeled the "official language of Gyarong" (C: *Jiarong guanhua*; T: *Rgyal Rong skad*). So far, scholars have not reached agreement on the academic classification of this language. Some contend that since its vocabulary, expressions, and pronunciation are close to ancient or classical Tibetan,[11] it is the oldest existing Tibetan language. Others claim instead that it is a subcategory of the Tibetan language family (Luo and Fu 1954; Qu 1984). Some hold that it is an independent language category parallel with Tibetan in the Tibeto-Burman language family (Lin Xiangrong 1993). And finally, some maintain that it belongs to the Qiangic language of this same family.[12]

There are several other major distinctive languages/dialects spoken by the remaining Gyarongwa: Ergong, Amdo, and Khampa dialects as well as the Qiang language. Some scholars assert that Ergong should be classified as a distinctive language in relation to the "official" Gyarong language (Sun Hongkai 1983; Huang Bufan 1988), but others claim that it is the western dialect of the "official" language (Qu 1990; Lin Xiangrong 1993). Most nomads in Gyarong speak the nomadic Amdo Tibetan dialect, while many other local residents speak a Khampa Tibetan dialect. The Suopo people I worked with speak this Khampa dialect, and a little more than one-third of the total Zangzu population in Danba uses it (Lin Junhua 2006b). A group of people in today's Heishui County in Aba Tibetan and Qiang Autonomous Prefecture speak the Qiang language, but they don't identify themselves as Qiangzu, an officially recognized independent ethnic group in China. Instead they have often been classified—though vaguely—as Gyarongwa.

Therefore, Gyarong's ethnolinguistic map is very complicated. Since the majority of Gyarong's population speak either the "official" language or Ergong, communicating with other Zangzu is nearly impossible. Even those who speak a dialect that is recognized by scholars as a Khampa one have difficulty conversing with people from other Kham regions because of their distinctive accent. Yet, since the Suopowa and others in Danba who speak this Khampa dialect are so embedded in Gyarong—a region that is popularly perceived to be geographically and culturally close to the Han—many Khampa Tibetans don't even count their native tongue as a Khampa dialect or even as a version of Tibetan. This holds true even though there is a substantial variety of dialects among different groups of Khampa Tibetans, who also have considerable trouble understanding one another. This reveals the power of popular images of Gyarong distinctiveness among Tibetans and how little these images have been affected by the arguments of scholars and linguists.

Tsanlha Ngawang from Gyarong, a scholar of classical Tibetan and Gyarong language and history, has continued to argue in our conversations that the "official" Gyarong language is the closest to ancient Tibetan and that this fully demonstrates the truth of the Gyarongwa's Tibetan status. However, his influence is limited to the academic field, and his scholarship has not had much effect on the generally disapproving attitude of other Zangzu toward the Gyarong dialect and the Gyarongwa's Tibetan identity.

If the Gyarongwa's Tibetan origin and identity are ambiguous and disputable, why did the central government reidentify them as Zangzu in 1954? This may have happened in part because, despite the historical and linguistic ambiguity, Tibetan cultural elements in Gyarong are easily visible to outsiders. Religion is the strongest Tibetan element that has been highlighted by the Gyarongwa and other Tibetans. By the 1950s, almost the entire Gyarong population was either Tibetan Buddhist or Bon. As in other parts of Tibet, most households sent at least one male child to the monastery to become a monk. Monks, particularly reincarnate or learned lamas, enjoyed very high esteem among the nobles and the general public. Monks who learned scripture well and/or who had financial resources, especially those from the Gelugpa tradition, or Yellow Hat Sect, would normally be sent by their families and monastery for further study at one of the three major Gelugpa monasteries in Lhasa (Ganden, Drepung, and Sera). The returnees, particularly those who managed to earn the highest monastic degree of *geshe*, automatically gained tremendous respect among the Gyarongwa. Other easily recognizable Tibetan elements include architecture, traditional foods such as tea, yak butter, and *tsampa* (roasted barley flour),[13] and certain customs that are normally religious in nature, such as mountain worship and the celebration of Tibetan religious festivals. Therefore, the work team the central government sent for its ethnic identification project couldn't deny Gyarong's Tibetanness, although the locals were temporarily identified as an independent ethnic group, Gyarongzu, based largely on the team's classification of the Gyarong language as distinctive.

Some of Gyarong's former nobles who had become important high-ranking officials in the newly founded Sichuan Tibetan Autonomous Region (today's Aba Tibetan and Qiang Autonomous Prefecture) insisted that Gyarong had been part of the Tibetan ethnic group since ancient times and simultaneously affirmed that the Gyarongwa shared cultural traditions (religion) and lifestyle with other Tibetans, despite the work team's explanations and linguistic categorizations. Eventually, the central government agreed to change its ethnic label from "Gyarongzu" to "Zangzu." In the early 1950s, the political situation was still volatile and a number of rebellions had arisen in Tibetan and other regions. Thus, support from those who had been *tusi* and nobles, and still had the loyalty of their former subjects and commoners, was essential for the Party's maintenance of stability in Tibetan regions. This compromise awakened both the Gyarongwa's consciousness as Zangzu and their sense of marginalization among Zangzu.

In point of fact, the ethnic identification project has had a very profound impact on officially identified ethnic minorities and on ethnic relations in China. One direct consequence is that people from segregated villages and regions who had limited contact with other groups or people who were rarely conscious of being an integrated ethnic community were now "unified" under an ethnic umbrella created by the state (see, e.g., on the Zhuang, Kaup 2000). Before the 1950s, Tibetan societies were so diversified that they had a limited sense of shared political, national, or even religious identity. Except for Central Tibet, which was literally a unified political entity under the Dalai Lama and the Tibetan Kashag government, other Tibetan regions, including Gyarong, had been ruled separately by more than eight hundred *tusi* as well as by officials dispatched by the Nationalist regime. In Gyarong, the whole region was traditionally under the control of a number of *tusi*, but by the early twentieth century, all the official titles of Gyarong *tusi* had been rescinded by either the Qing court or the subsequent Nationalist regime, which established administrative units in Gyarong and designated or appointed their own officials to govern the region. In reality, however, most *tusi* retained considerable power in their territory and continued to exist until 1950, when the Chinese Communist Party finally abolished the system.

Although the Dalai Lama's spiritual influence went far beyond the Central Tibetan region, there were varying degrees of discord and the development of separate identities among different schools of Tibetan Buddhism, not to mention between the believers of the Bon religion and those of Tibetan Buddhism. The three principal Tibetan subgroups—Central (Ü-Tsang) Tibetans, Amdo Tibetans, and Khampa Tibetans—were also mutually exclusive to the extent that even today many Central Tibetans don't recognize people from Amdo and Kham as Tibetans or "authentic" Tibetans. Due to linguistic and other differences, the Gyarongwa had developed even less collective identity in relation to any of these Tibetan groups.

Therefore, in a real sense, it was the Chinese central government that created a unified Tibetan nationality. With the awakening of an ethno-national identity among all peoples labeled "Zangzu," a popular conception began to evolve among those designated as such. According to this ethnic stereotype, Zangzu share a common origin, a glorious history, and a set of cultural traditions, and the bonds among the various subgroups have never been weakened. This perception has given rise to a Tibetan ethno-nationalism that is not necessarily about Tibetan independence. It is often just a sense of pride and reaffirmation of Zangzu uniqueness and unity. Many Zangzu, particularly intellectuals and lamas, take delight in the idea that the Zangzu have a "superior" culture and traditions vis-à-vis the Han and others due largely to the great tradition of Tibetan Buddhism, which they characterize as a faith of profundity and compassion. This pride has much to do with the influence of the Dalai Lama, whose reputation as one of the most important spiritual leaders in the world has convinced most Zangzu of the vitality and supremacy of Tibetan Buddhism.

Most Gyarongwa share this pride, too. They are proud of being members of this great ethnic group and of having such a charismatic and world-renowned spiritual head. However, the Gyarongwa's distinctiveness still makes them stand out as "different" from other Zangzu. Since, in the view of some Zangzu, the Gyarongwa are actually culturally close to the Han or very much Sinicized, they are sometimes seen by other Zangzu to be pro-Han and thus pro–Chinese government.

The Gyarongwa are often confronted with questions about their cultural identity and their relationship with the Han, as I can illustrate from my own experience. On an afternoon in March 2009, after shopping at Wuhouci[14] in Chengdu, the capital of Sichuan, a lama friend and I were looking for a taxi to take us to Kangding, the capital of Ganzi Tibetan Autonomous Prefecture. While we were walking to a hotel where many drivers from Ganzi prefecture park their cars, two young Tibetan men stopped us, inquiring in Tibetan, "Are you going to Kangding?" After we answered in the affirmative, they asked where we were from.

I said, "We are from Danba."

They seemed somewhat surprised and asked, "Why can you speak Tibetan?"

My friend replied, "Isn't the Gyarong language Tibetan, too? It is an ancient dialect. We [our ancestors] used to speak the same language."

Then these two men told us that their car would head for Kangding "in just a short while." As my friend and I were chatting with each other while we were waiting, a Tibetan woman came up and asked the drivers when they were leaving. One man whispered that they might not leave until the next morning if they were unable to get enough passengers. I told them that we couldn't wait any longer, and they asked what we would do then. My friend said that we would go to Baigongling Bus Station to purchase tickets and leave from there for Danba directly the next morning. The following conversation then took place between one of the two Tibetan men (A) and my friend (B):

A: Why do you want to go there? Do you want to go there to stay at a Han hotel, eat their food, and take their bus?

B: Whether it is a Han bus or a Tibetan bus, it is the only bus that will take us back to Danba. . . .

A: You Danba people just love the Han. Whatever they do, you will follow.

B: What do you mean? You hate the Han? What clothes are you wearing [they were wearing Han-style clothes]? Do you love hot pot [a typical Sichuan food popular with Tibetans]? You don't eat Sichuan food at all? Don't treat us like this. Aren't we the same [Tibetans]?

Seeing the atmosphere heating up, I stopped my friend, and we left. But he was still upset, saying that "many [Tibetan] nomadic people are just like this. They don't know much. They are not really open-minded. They just say that we are not Tibetan. It is not good to have such divisions among us."

This attitude toward the Gyarongwa is not unusual. Some Zangzu complained that the Gyarongwa didn't stand behind other Zangzu in the Tibet riots in 2008 and instead acted "as if nothing had happened." In early 2006 in various Tibetan regions, people started to burn otter, leopard, tiger, and fox pelts, which they had normally used for their hats, clothes, and adornments. This action came in response to the Dalai Lama's call for an end to the killing of wild animals and the illegal wildlife trade by Tibetans at the Kalachakra ceremony held in Amaravati, Andhra Pradesh, India, in January 2006. However, nothing happened in most Gyarong regions. A lot of Gyarongwa continued to purchase these pelts and wear such "fancy" clothes. Later I heard many complaints from other Zangzu who couldn't figure out "what was wrong with the Gyarongwa." According to my lama friend, a well-respected Buddhist master, the Gyarongwa were "too practical" and too concerned about "secular stuff" and didn't devote themselves to religious matters as much as other Zangzu. This view is shared by many Gyarongwa and other Zangzu, although it is hard to measure what is "too practical" and "too secular."

As in all other Tibetan regions, most monasteries in Gyarong were destroyed during and after the Democratic Reform (Minzhu Gaige) of the late 1950s. Although the 1980s saw a vigorous religious revival, the restoration of monasteries and religion per se in Gyarong was less impressive than in most other Tibetan regions. As a result, the importance of monasteries as well as Tibetan religions proper in local society has decreased to varying degrees in most parts of Gyarong. Besides political control and limited funding as well as perceivable Sinicizing processes,[15] the lack of systematic monastic training and the scarcity of important religious figures and learned lamas in Gyarong is a major factor in the dilution of religious identity among many Gyarongwa. Before the 1950s, it was a general practice for monks to go to Lhasa and important temples in other Tibetan areas for further learning, and when some of them came back with prestigious religious degrees, they usually had a significant influence on the general public and even nobles. It was not until the early 1980s that this practice resumed. However, the government continued to regulate and monitor the activities of monasteries and monks, and it discouraged monks from traveling far to mix with those from other Tibetan regions in the name of learning scripture. The systematic monastic training in Lhasa and many other places was not fully restored either. As a result, after the old learned lamas passed away, they were replaced by young monks who lacked sophisticated monastic training and thus did not have their elders' influence. This is the problem faced by most monasteries in Gyarong. I have heard many complaints from Gyarong villagers about the lack of great lamas in their region. Without important and charismatic religious figures, the Gyarongwa's faith in the monasteries and religion has been seriously affected.

With esteemed religious figures, how would the situation be different? Maerkang ('Bar Khams), the capital of Aba Tibetan and Qiang Autonomous Prefecture, is a cultural hub in the Gyarong region. Many locals there have very strong religious beliefs. This is probably due to the fact that, since the 1980s, some elderly monks who fled to India in 1959 have come back and a number of children and youth have found their way to India to learn scripture there. Some of them were able to return after years of rigorous monastic training. Despite the political control and surveillance, the returnees and other lamas have been able to renovate or rebuild quite a few monasteries and establish monastic schools where they can train novices, thanks to tremendous support from local villagers, businessmen, and even officials and cadres.[16] The reason for this enthusiastic local support has to do not only with the locals' religious beliefs and their desire for the restoration and development of religion in this region; it is also linked to the shining example set by learned lamas. These lamas' mastery of religious philosophy, personal decorum, and charisma has exerted great influence on the locals' perceptions of religion and thus on their religious identity.[17] For instance, several years ago, a village head in Maerkang told me that many village parents let their children quit elementary school in order to attend a local monastery because these parents were frustrated that the boys didn't learn "good things" from school—they often fought among themselves, played truant, didn't do their homework, and didn't help much at home after school. Just several months after having been sent to the monastery, they were transformed: they started to work hard, talk politely to the elderly, and care for their parents. He attributed these positive changes to the influence of great masters at this monastery. Later I heard many similar claims about the significant influence of outstanding lamas on the local community. As a result, local religious identities have been reinforced. However, in many parts of the Gyarong region, the lack of such charismatic religious figures has taken a toll on religious identity.

The dilution of religious identity for the Gyarongwa is a complicated issue. In other Zangzu regions, there has been anxiety about the negative effect the Party's Zangzu and religious policies and modern forces like commercialization and tourism have had on religious identity, but the situation is extreme in Gyarong. This shift toward secularization marginalizes the Gyarongwa among Zangzu, as Tibetanness often boils down to demonstrating reverence for the Dalai Lama. Zangzu are united as a close-knit whole by their tremendous love for this great leader, so the Gyarongwa's "indifference" to the call of the spiritual leader and less devotion to religious matters disqualify them as "authentic" Tibetans in the eyes of other Zangzu.

Suopo's case is even more complicated. The majority of the Suopowa practice the Bon religion. Bon is an indigenous religion in Tibet, but with the rise of Buddhism in the eighth century, it suffered serious setbacks. When Bon priests eventually lost their ground in Central Tibet, some escaped to Gyarong. With the support and patronage of local kings, Bon flourished in Gyarong. However, in the late eighteenth century, Emperor Qianlong of the Qing dynasty ordered the eradication of the Bon religion in Dajinchuan (today's Jinchuan County) and Xiaojinchuan (today's Xiaojin County). He labeled Bon a "vicious cult" (xiejiao) because it had "colluded" with local kings against the Qing troops dispatched to subdue the rebellions and had the Gelugpa replace the Bon (see Peng 2003). Although the Qing court didn't take such drastic measures against those Bon Gyarong kings who were not involved in the rebellions, this policy of advocating Buddhism while curbing Bon in Gyarong signaled the further erosion of Bon's status. The situation remains unchanged today. Thus, due to the disparity in influence wielded by Buddhism and Bon, many common Tibetan Buddhists accuse Bon of "heresy," with some even claiming that Bon is "un-Tibetan" or not Tibetan enough—an ironic assertion considering that Bon is the indigenous religion of Tibet. When the Suopowa seek temporary employment in other Khampa counties in Ganzi Tibetan Autonomous Prefecture, many don't reveal their religious background for fear of discrimination.

These examples show that although the Gyarongwa are officially recognized as Zangzu, their Tibetan identity has been constantly challenged and disputed. But how do the Gyarongwa look at and evaluate their relationship with other Tibetans? In my interviews with dozens of Gyarong villagers, nearly all expressed the idea that they are "different from other Tibetans." The most frequently mentioned difference is language, followed by cultural differences, especially the "wildness" of Tibetan men from Kham or nomadic regions, whom they believed to be short-tempered and easily provoked into fisticuffs or even knife fights. They also mentioned the male supremacy or "male chauvinism" of "typical" Tibetan men who don't help much with household chores and treat their wives badly, in contrast with Gyarong men, who do most of the heavy labor at home and care more for their wives. Another common opinion is that other Tibetans are usually too religious, having an almost fervent faith in their lamas and spending excessive amounts of money and time on religious matters. Sanitation and foods were frequently mentioned, too. In these villagers' views, "typical" Tibetans, especially nomads, are not clean and don't care much about cleanliness in clothing, food, and housing. They also commented on the fact that nomads eat very simple traditional food like tea, yak butter, *tsampa*, and yak or mutton and don't even know how to cook properly. However, not everything about "typical" Tibetans or nomads was negative. Some of the villagers who have had frequent contact with the former argued that they are straightforward, honest, and, once friendship was established, trustworthy and loyal, unlike "sophisticated" and "practical" farmers, including the Gyarongwa. Nevertheless, on the whole, these villagers' portrayal of Tibetans and nomads, who were said to be too "uncultivated," "conservative" (regarding men's attitude toward women), overreligious, and unclean, expressed a sense of superiority.

In contrast, from the perspective of many Gyarong elites with whom I interacted—including state employees, scholars, teachers, lamas, and others—despite differences between the Gyarongwa and other Zangzu, what really mattered was that they were all Tibetans. Like my lama friend, these elites were frustrated with other Zangzu's demeaning attitude toward the Gyarongwa. But from my friend's point of view, this attitude arose from ignorance of the fact that the Gyarong language and culture are classified as among the most authentic subcategories of Tibetan language and culture. Thus, authenticating the Gyarongwa's Tibetanness has become a great concern. Tsanlha Ngawang's proposition that the "official" Gyarong language is the ancient, classic Tibetan and that Gyarong has always been part of the Tibetan ethnicity was quite influential and well received in academic circles, where he was much respected for its erudition and rigorous reasoning. Some Han and Zangzu scholars with whom I am personally acquainted have been convinced by his works and have used some of his concepts to buttress similar claims. But beyond the academic field, do common Gyarong villagers care about their Tibetan identity at all? Or do they make an effort to prove their Tibetanness?

In general, the Gyarongwa are fully conscious of their status as Zangzu, the label imprinted not only on their registration records and ID cards but also in their minds, thanks to the ethnic identification project and ethnic policy implemented by the state. They identify themselves with other Zangzu as "a single unity," but only with increasing interactions with outsiders—Tibetans, Han, and tourists—has the issue of how to best represent themselves and reconfigure Gyarong-Tibetan relations become an immediate and important concern to the common Gyarongwa. As indicated above, when encountering other Zangzu, the Gyarongwa tend to highlight their common Tibetan identity, and from time to time, some do so by concealing their Gyarongness and Bon background. When the Gyarongwa interact with the Han in Han regions, they may just claim their Zangzu status, since most Han have little knowledge of Gyarong. However, when tourists come to Gyarong, locals are faced with inquiries about their relations with other Zangzu because local dress and customs are different from what tourists expect to find among Tibetans. Several local guides and villagers in Danba consulted me on Tibet-Gyarong relations as well as other issues on Tibetan and local history because they didn't know how to answer tourists' questions.

In their interactions with tourists, they have developed "standard" interpretations of Tibetan and local history and culture, assuring tourists that they are not only authentic Tibetans but also the most unique Tibetan subgroup. They take pride in their Tibetan heritage but realize that the local culture is what tourists come for and so immerse themselves in it. In this way, they not only subvert other Zangzu's discourse of their non-Tibetan identity but also assert their uniqueness among the Zangzu subgroups.

The Suopo case is even more distinctive. The Suopowa speak a Khampa dialect; thus, many of them claim that they are real Tibetans, unlike other Gyarongwa who speak various non-Tibetan languages. However, as mentioned, their assertion is not usually accepted by other Khampa people. As a result, a paradox emerges: some Suopowa feel that they are marginalized by other Khampa people for their "impure" Tibetan language and "contaminated" Tibetan blood, while the Suopowa feel superior to other Gyarongwa because of their "purer" Tibetan blood. The Suopowa are aware that their Bon religious beliefs further disqualify them as "authentic" Tibetans in the eyes of some "radical" Tibetans. In an effort to subvert this negative stereotyping, Suopo elites constantly reminded me and other outsiders that Bon in Suopo has taken such a broad-minded approach that it coexists peacefully with Buddhism.[18] An example of this harmonious relationship is said to be the locals' great reverence for Berotsana, a renowned translator and master of Buddhist scripture and one of the first seven monks ordained in Tibet. Berotsana was banished to Gyarong by anti-Buddhist forces in the court of King Trisong Detsen in the eighth century. After arriving in Gyarong, he started to propagate Buddhism and gathered a large following (Dmu Dge 1997), although one might logically expect that the Suopowa or Bon believers would have had a strong animosity toward this Buddhist master. Suopo elites suggest that local admiration for Berotsana reveals the tolerant open-mindedness of both the Bon religion and the Suopowa. In doing so, they seriously challenge the degraded portrayal of Bon and assert their sense of pride in this liberal religion.

In their campaign for recognition, the Suopowa, especially elites, have also long denied the translation of the place-name Suopo (T: Sog Po), which in "standard" Tibetan means "Mongols." This interpretation suggests that the Suopowa are descendants of Mongols, who were said to have come and settled in the area in the thirteenth and fourteenth centuries (see, e.g., Wang Huailin 2006). Suopo elites oppose this explanation, declaring that they have nothing in common with Mongols and thus proclaiming their "unadulterated" Tibetan origin and culture.

The Suopowa's reactions toward perceived negative labels suggest that their Khampa or Tibetan identity is insecure and that they must find a counterexample, other Gyarongwa with "impure" Tibetan blood, to serve as a foil in order to authenticate their claim. Suopo possesses a unique resource in the stone watchtowers that have become a well-known tourist site in China and which Suopo elites and villagers assert is the most unique and invaluable representation of the best of Tibetan architecture throughout all the Zangzu regions. Suopo has 175 remaining watchtowers that are hundreds of years old and make up nearly one-third of the total number of such buildings in Danba County. Due to their important historical and cultural value, the Chinese government has nominated them for World Heritage status.[19] These exquisite and imposing high-rise structures stand in the breathtaking landscape of Suopo, making them a magnet for tourists. The Suopowa make use of the towers as an example of both their distinctiveness and their Tibetanness. They also take pride in their folk songs and dances as being the most unique and thus the most "authentic" in Danba, Gyarong, and even the whole Zangzu region. These forms of heritage, however, can also be found in Gyarong and other Zangzu areas. It is the ruins of the palace of the matriarchal Eastern Queendom as well as the supposed queendom traditions that set Suopo above all the rest.

## Chapter 2

## MASCULINE AND FEMININE
## INTERNAL OTHERS IN CHINA

＊

One of the paradoxes in the queendom discourse is the elevation of the Suopowa's feminine image along with their assertion of Khampa Tibetan masculinity. Although concerns and interests are manifested in this approach, their self-representation is not merely a matter of free choice, and it is shaped by a well-established framework of ethnic representations rooted in both the official and popular discourses in China. Minority representations also often reflect state agendas and tourist capital and interests. The roots of the Zangzu villagers' dedication to the queendom cause and their motives for self-feminization are evident in the landscape of ethnic representations and in the official and popular discourses of ethnic Others that inform sociopolitical change and ethnic relations in China.

What has characterized and come out of minority representations is that ethnicity is sexualized by the fact that minority members are often identified with such images as "oversexed," "promiscuous," "hypermasculine," and "hyperfeminine." At the same time, sexuality is ethnicized, since these same labels are often reserved predominantly or exclusively for minority members who become the testing ground for the "standard" performances of different categories of sexuality under the umbrella of "masculinity" or "femininity."[1] Two significant cases of minority representations will be introduced here for the purpose of examining, on the one hand, how sexualized ethnicity and ethnicized sexuality play out and, on the other, how each of these two cases—a "masculinized" image of Mongols and a "feminized" image of the "Women's Country" at Lugu Lake in Yunnan, in southwest China—serves as a prelude to the discussion of the Eastern Queendom, in which both masculinity and femininity inform the local villagers' struggle for the queendom label.

## WOLFISH OTHERS VERSUS SHEEPISH HAN

In the preface to a collection of folk songs from Hunan, Guizhou, and Yunnan provinces in which minority groups have a strong presence, Wen Yiduo, one of the most influential and outspoken poets of the New Cultural Movement generation, wrote: "You say these [poems] are primitive and savage. You are right, and that is just what we need today. We've been civilized too long, and now we have nowhere left to go. We shall have to pull out the last and purest card, and release the animal nature that has lain dormant in us for several thousand years, so that we can bite back" (quoted in Oakes 1997, 67–68). This is the representative voice of the New Cultural Movement (1917–23), characterized by a radical intellectual break with the past, and it asserts that China should absorb vital energy and strength from uncorrupted and "wild" Others in order to remove the suffocating yokes of semicolonialism and feudal dogmas of Confucianism and gain entry to the modern world.[2] In this portrayal, the Han civilization per se is believed to be the fundamental cause of China's degeneration and the reason it has become the prey of bullying Western powers—that is, Confucianism has stifled the animal nature and wild instinct of the Han, and thus both Han bodies and minds were weakened and emasculated, putting China in a very disadvantaged position in the face of the militaristic and aggressive West.

Such concern and anxiety is resounding again in China at the turn of the twenty-first century, a time of intensified reforms, increasing influence in the world, and skyrocketing nationalism rooted in popular longing for the restoration of China's great glory. The most representative work of this endeavor is the autobiographical novel *Wolf Totem* (Lang tuteng)—one of the best-selling and most influential literary works in China in the first decade of the twenty-first century—which claims that only the "wolf spirits" of nomadic people can cure China's "civilization malady." This book has created tremendous controversy and stirred heated debate among its millions of Han and minority readers in China. Many speak highly of its ideas as offering a solution to China's intrinsic problem, but it also receives enormous criticism for its romanticization or untruthful representations of Mongols and its irrational and excessive degrading of Chinese civilization.

## WHY *WOLF TOTEM?*

*Wolf Totem* comes at a time of an aggravated crisis of masculinity as well as rising nationalism in China. The calls for restoring masculinity among Chinese youth and in nationalist discourse occur side by side. The discourse about masculinity is embedded in China's desire to become a predominant world power and the Chinese public's wholehearted embrace of this ambitious agenda. These Chinese nationalist aspirations are often conveyed and exhibited through masculinized expressions, such as assertiveness, determination, strong bodies, fearlessness, perseverance, and, above all, virility—the very qualities that are often associated with dominant males.

There is increasing concern about the emasculation of the younger male generation in China. Many intellectuals and the general public express great worry about boys and male youth taking on "weak" and "fragile" personalities that are unassertive, highly dependent, emotional or sensitive, and timid. As to the reason, most scholars are inclined to attribute it to the feminization of preschool and primary school education, meaning that the majority of teachers and instructors in pre-secondary schools and even in secondary schools are female, especially in urban settings. It is said that the problem with such an unbalanced sex ratio among school faculty is that male students are insulated from the virility, courage, determination, and optimism that a male teacher can transmit and inspire in them, while female teachers, serving as authority figures and role models, pass on feminine qualities like sensitivity and tenderness.[3] More than that, an intrinsic problem in the Chinese educational system is believed to evolve from the flawed educational philosophy that attaches too much importance to collective discipline and exams rather than (male) individuality—that is, obedience (*tinghua*) and examination scores are often the most important criteria in evaluating students as "good" or "bad." Many boys who are "hyperactive" or "naughty" at school, and thus don't do well on their homework and exams, are susceptible to being labeled "bad students" by teachers. As a result, many of these students become so frustrated with the negative image that they conform to the school norms at the cost of their virile "nature" (*tianxing*) (Wu Wenyu 2008; Sun, Li, and Zhao 2010).

Another important factor is that China's one-child policy led to parents (and also grandparents) spoiling their only child to the extent that all children are raised like daughters who have received too much attention and emotional support, which results in overdependence, timidity, and hypersensitivity.[4] Some scholars also attribute feminization to the lack of the dominant male figure in family education (Han 2007). The patriarchal family structure in China is to be blamed for this because the father is traditionally associated with the role of breadwinner while the mother is assigned the duty of taking care of and educating the children. As a result, boys are believed to become "demasculinized" through their mothers' excessive care and fondness.[5]

Feminized boys are seen as an obstacle to China's rise, apart from the negative judgment of their sexuality and their "confused" or inverted gender roles. Since feminization is seen as a tendency among the younger male generation throughout the country, especially in urban settings, these feminized children—the pillar and backbone of China's future—seem unable to fulfill their responsibility for the country's revival and prosperity, as their "weak" personalities lack virility and the strength to face challenges and overcome difficulties (Sun Yunxiao 1993; Sun, Li, and Zhao 2010). Besides the spiritual or personality weakness of the younger generation, many of its members are also physically weak, due largely to the lack of physical exercise and sports. As a matter of fact, in China, the "sickly bodies" image is often linked mostly with intellectuals who are the equivalent of the "pallid-faced scholars" (*baimian shusheng*)[6] of old times (Brownell 1995).

What is the relationship between a weak body and a weak mind? There are two explanations: one says that although a weak body cannot be translated into a weak mind directly, those with weak minds are inclined to have weak bodies, and vice versa; the other suggests that a weak body will definitely bring about a weak mind or that a weak mind always goes together with a weak body. Chen Duxiu, a leading figure in the New Culture Movement, cofounder of the Chinese Community Party, and an advocate for the latter explanation, once commented: "Every time when I encounter the intellectual youth, who are too weak to truss up a chicken, too spineless to assert virility as a man, with pallid face and slim waist, as effeminate as virgins, and as feeble as the sick, [then I cannot help thinking that] counting on such physically and mentally weak citizens, how is it possible for them to take great responsibilities?" (Chen Duxiu 1915).

In this way, the bodies and minds of nationals become the index and point of reference in Chinese nationalist discourse. A strong nation requires strong bodies and minds. The West and/or Japan were the models for China in that they were believed to have successfully integrated these two aspects in their national characters and thus were empowered to dominate other nations. China was weak during its "unhappy" encounters with Western powers beginning in the first half of the nineteenth century and the New Culture Movement in the early twentieth century, and, in the eyes of some Chinese intellectuals, this situation remains true—China continues to suffer from its "weak" national character exemplified by weak bodies and minds. Therefore, the weakened bodies and emasculated minds of the younger generation in China pose a great challenge to China's ascension to the rank of the great world powers.

Then what is the fundamental cause of these weak bodies and minds? The New Culture Movement intellectuals and other progressive or reform-minded intellectuals attribute this to the corrupted feudal system or Confucianism, which "esteems literacy and despises martiality" (*zhongwen qingwu*), as the Chinese Communist Party did and still does. Physical exercises and sports are also important components of martiality in a broad sense in China (Brownell 1995). Therefore, many of these intellectuals— including Wen Yiduo, Chen Duxiu, and Jiang Rong, the author of *Wolf Totem*—have called for the revival of the "animal nature" and virility of the Han that have been stifled by Confucianism and traditional values. Only when this animal nature is restored can the Chinese nation be reinvigorated, achieve a privileged status in this world, and regain its long-lost glory.

It is believed that not only Western Others but also Internal Others are endowed with such virile attributes. Thus, for some intellectuals, those "wild" minorities who have maintained their "natural instincts" in harsh environments and under tough conditions are also models for the Han. As a result, the status of minorities is transformed from being on the periphery to being at the symbolic center in the sense that minorities are needed to reconstruct and masculinize the Han-self by transmitting their "wild" energies to the Han. Nevertheless, the centralizing of minorities in Chinese national discourse also reflects their challenge to the hegemonic Han-self (see Gladney 1991).

## Wolf Totem

*Wolf Totem* is an example of this tendency. It is an autobiographical novel in that it is based on the author's experience of living for more than a decade in the Inner Mongolian grassland. It also expresses his perspective on the wolves' role in sustaining the ecological system of the grassland, the nomadic lifestyle and national spirit of the Mongols, and the Mongols' significance to the rejuvenation of Chinese civilization. It also contains his reflections on Han chauvinism and shortsighted governmental agendas. The author's points of view are elucidated by the two protagonists: Chen Zhen and Yang Ke. These two young students from Beijing are sent down to Inner Mongolia during the Cultural Revolution (1966–76) to be "reeducated by the great masses" in response to Chairman Mao's call for urban students, referred to as "intellectual youth" (*zhishi qingnian*, or *zhiqing* for short) to go "up to the mountains and down to the countryside." In the book, the two students, especially Chen Zhen, go through a dramatic transformation, from Han-centric students whose fear and hatred of wolves were rooted in the "petty peasant mentality" of the Han to spiritually reborn Mongolian men and worshippers of the Wolf Totem.

In Han folklore and popular expressions, wolves are the most evil and atrocious of animals. Consequently, as Chen phrases it, "We [Han] call the most malicious people wolves; we call sex fiends wolves; we say the greediest people have the appetite of a wolf; the American imperialists are referred to as ambitious wolves; and any time an adult wants to frighten a child, he cries out 'Wolf!'" (Jiang 2008, 271–72). With this notion ingrained in their minds, the revolutionary cadres in Olonbulga, where the story is set, and the Ujimchin Banner in Inner Mongolia (both places populated by the Han and Sinicized Mongols who have "forgotten their roots") blame wolves for inflicting massive damage on their herds and embark on a large-scale campaign of exterminating wolves "until every Olonbulag wolf is dead" (201). Like other Han, Chen has an instinctual aversion to wolves at first. As time goes on, however, he comes to realize that wolves play an indispensable role in safeguarding the grassland and are part of the Mongols' identities, and thus the extermination of wolves would mean the complete destruction of the grassland and the Mongolian nomadic way of life. But that is not all. The Han and the government would pay a great price for their destructive acts because the environmental deterioration of the Mongolian grassland would have a devastating impact on northern China, including Beijing. Furthermore, destruction of the nomadic way of life and grassland would mean that China would lose the stronghold for its revitalization.

In Chen's close observations, he discovers that wolves possess the admirable qualities of courage, wisdom, cooperation, organization, discipline, patience, and perseverance, as well as deference to authority and defiance of inhospitable conditions. After having understood this, the Mongolian troops' crushing military victories in history and the invincible robustness of Genghis Khan and his descendants are no longer a mystery for him, and he is convinced that the wolves had trained the Mongols through their encounters and mutual struggles to be the most skillful, intrepid, and formidable warriors and fighters in the world. Wild animals, such as gazelles, field mice, ground squirrels, hares, and marmots, and livestock such as cattle, sheep, and horses would overgraze and destroy the grassland without the wolves to check their uncontrolled growth by killing them. Wolves also ward off epidemics or plagues and purify the grassland by quickly disposing of the dead bodies of animals killed by natural disasters. Therefore, wolves have a unique place in the Mongols' lives and form an intricate and intimate relationship with the nomads: on the one hand, both sides constantly battle each other as people try to protect their livestock from these insatiable predators, and in confronting their powerful rivals, Mongols have cultivated outstanding combat skills and remarkable virility; on the other hand, the Mongols regard the wolves as protectors of the grassland and as their totem. This relationship constitutes the spiritual core of the grassland civilization, manifested in the Mongols' broad-minded attitude of living with nature rather than struggling to overcome it. As a result, the Mongols' formidable virility is "rational virility" rather than "savage virility." The latter is a partial or incorrect representation of Mongolian virility that is often associated with bloody ferocity and crude brutality, but instead, the virility of the Mongols is balanced by their profound understanding of nature and respect for life.

In comparison, Chen realizes, the Han civilization is rooted in agrarian culture characterized by a narrow-minded "petty peasant mentality" (*xiao-nong yishi*). This mentality has resulted in conservative outlooks, a lack of pioneering spirit, self-importance, and, above all, a weak and submissive national character. The situation is exacerbated by the detrimental impact of Confucianism embedded in agrarian culture, and the two are intertwined to define the Han-self and national character. According to Jiang, at its very beginning, Confucianism embraced the elements of virility and robustness due to its origin in the seminomadic environment, but it has developed to an extreme since the eleventh century, when its focus on "maintaining the heavenly principle and eradicating human desire" (*cun tianli mie renyu*) was promulgated. If the goal were to eradicate human desire, there would be no place for a "wolfish nature" at all. In essence, this ideology was designed to mold people into submissive and loyal subjects who would not object to the status quo. Therefore, the wolfish nature of nomadic people posed a serious challenge to the ruling order and had to be disputed and demonized. As a result, the wolfish nature of the Han, who evolved from nomadic life, has been stifled, and people have become so docile and soft that a "sheepish nature" has almost come to define the Han national character. Consequently, China has been bullied or overwhelmed by foreign powers who have managed to maintain their wolfish nature while developing sophisticated sociopolitical systems and advanced technologies. Thus, in the novel, Chen refers to the West and Japan as "civilized wolves." So in order to change the contemporary world order and rejuvenate itself, China must learn from the West and Japan and especially from its own Internal Others, masculinize the national discourse, and shed the sheepish character of its people. Mongols are the best potential mentors for the Han, yet instead of learning from the Mongols, the Han have spared no effort in attempting to destroy the grassland and the Mongols' masculine, nomadic way of life. *Wolf Totem* is a relentless critique of Han chauvinism and a sincere plea for the Han to become aware of this problem. Jiang describes in a strikingly vivid way the inferior and pitiful nature of the sheep:

> Sheep are truly stupid animals. When the wolf knocked the unfortunate sheep to the ground, the other sheep scattered in fright. But the entire flock soon calmed down, and there were even a few animals that timidly drew closer to watch the wolf eat a number of their flock. As they looked

on, more joined them, until at least a hundred sheep had virtually penned the wolf and its bloody victim in; they pushed and shoved and craned their necks to get a better look. Their expressions seemed to say, "Well, the wolf is eating you and not me!" Either that or, "You are dying so I can live." Their fear was measured by a sense of gloating. None made a move to stop the wolf.

Startled by the scene, Chen was reminded of the writer Lu Xun, who had written about a crowd of dull-witted Chinese looking on as a Japanese swordsman was about to lop off the head of a Chinese prisoner. What was the difference between that and this? No wonder the nomads see the Han Chinese as sheep. A wolf eating a sheep may be abhorrent, but far more loathsome were cowardly people who acted like sheep. (Jiang 2008, 319)

What a dramatic scene this is! Lu Xun (1881–1936), one of the most influential writers in twentieth-century China, known for his sharp and penetrating satirical writing style, lamented the sheepish and slavish national character of the Han. Now Jiang Rong is revealing the same deplorable reality—that is to say, the problem of the soft Han character has never been resolved and continues to haunt China. Although socialist China has replaced (or attempted to replace) Confucianism with a Marxist-Leninist-Maoist creed as the state ideology and has sped up its industrialization and modernization process, state policy and popular conceptions are still rooted in the narrow-minded petty peasant mentality. The cadres in Olonbulag were trying to exterminate "evil" wolves and planning to turn the fertile grasslands into farmlands. Native nomads and "converted" Mongols like Chen and his friend Yang Ke couldn't resist this hegemonic policy openly, for their actions would be labeled as "local ethno-nationalism" (*difang minzu zhuyi*) or antirevolutionary.

At odds with the normative eulogy of the hegemonic Chinese civilization, the author argues that Confucianism and petty peasant mentality had almost rendered China powerless against invading foreign powers in the nineteenth and twentieth centuries. Therefore, it was not the Manchu rulers of the Qing dynasty who were to blame for the loss of sovereignty and cession of territory. According to this theory, if it had not been for the "blood transfusion" the Manchus gave to Chinese civilization as well as the residue of their wolfish nature, which was sustained to the end of the Qing dynasty, the three northeastern provinces, Xinjiang, and Tibet would be absent from China's map today. This declaration is not a simple challenge to the contemporary Chinese official discourse; it is a complete inversion. Jiang asserts that nomadic peoples, mainly Mongols and Manchus, have contributed much more than the Han to the preservation and continuation of Chinese civilization by constantly providing "wild" and vigorous new blood. The tragedy, however, is that the Han and the state have given these minorities little credit. On the contrary, they are demonized as barbarians or marginalized as ancillary to Chinese civilization rather than recognized as its mainstay and savior. The Party and the Han populace have not been aware of the fact that they are digging their own graves by exterminating wolves and destroying the grassland. If the Han do not act in time to halt their excessive appropriation of natural resources in the vast Inner Mongolian grassland and end the destructive act of turning it into farmland, there will be no way to recover from the loss of the last hope for China's revival or to repair the damage caused by desertification.

In pointing out the inherent "disease" of the Han, Jiang earnestly calls for the replacement of the Han sheepish nature with the wolfish nature that they can learn from the "superior" Mongols. Thus, the Han must bow to the Mongols as their serious and sincere students. Chen—the novel's protagonist (perhaps a stand-in for the author himself)—has succeeded in converting himself spiritually to Mongol values after realizing that his unmanliness and cowardliness have been firmly embedded in his Han blood: " 'I'm worse than useless,' Chen said with a sigh, deeply ashamed. 'Gutless as the sheep. A dog is worth more than me, not to mention a woman. Even a nine-year-old boy showed me up' " (Jiang 2008, 11).

Here, a Han person unprecedentedly positions himself as inferior to a Mongolian dog, a Mongolian woman, and a Mongolian boy, justifying the legitimacy of the Others as masters and superiors. An unpretentious and self-effacing attitude on the part of the Han is the key to learning the essence of the Mongols' wolfish nature, and only by being transfused with new Mongolian blood will China be able to strengthen and elevate itself into an unquestioned world power. In this way, Jiang has brought forward both an alternative to the normative discourse of the Han as civilizer and a reaffirmation and reinforcement of the indispensable role of virile and strong-willed Internal Others as the model for and holder of authenticity that the Han may resort to whenever necessary.

In all, *Wolf Totem* not only serves as a serious challenge to the Han-self but also suggests a way of ameliorating and perfecting Han-selfhood. In doing so, it imagines ethnic Others as existing for the Han, and their masculine image is appropriated for Han consumption and nationalist expression as well as for the reconstruction of Han-selfhood. In consequence, the identity of some ethnic Others is defined largely by "us" as masculine and tough in contrast to "our" effeteness and softness. Although it is true that in this book Mongols take pride in their virility while mocking Han "cowardliness" and "weakness," it is an outsider, Chen, who acts as the spokesman for the Mongols, whose voices would otherwise be silenced. It is still a Han who has taken the responsibility of telling "us" Han what "they" Mongols really are after having experienced personal rebirth and revitalization. Therefore, "their" identity continues to be represented through the lens of "us." Thus, "the use of the Other(s) to offer criticism of the self is not necessarily emancipatory for the represented Others," and, quite the contrary, the impact of the positive stereotyping "on the exoticized represented was often predictably the same—a prelude to control, dominance, and exploitation" (Anand 2007, 40–41). That being so, in essence the tribute to Mongolian virility reflects in inverted fashion the same asymmetric power relationship between the Han and ethnic Others as is embedded in both the official/state and popular discourses in China.

Thus, an examination of how such asymmetrical power is exhibited in these discourses and what implications it has for both Han-selfhood and Internal Others will present a general picture of the ethnic landscape in order to draw a sketch of dynamic ethnic relations in China. As much of the literature on the dominant-subordinate paradigm points out, the symbolization of asymmetrical power relations through gender imagery or sexual metaphor is usually a most effective tactic employed by the powerful to justify their advantaged standing by prioritizing their notion of sexuality and concept of masculinity/femininity as a norm or model.[7] This self-congratulatory stance puts identity politics in a place that is centered on the palpably oppositional characteristics transplanted from gender stereotypes and thus on conflicting identities imposed to fulfill the myth of rule by the "selected."[8] As will be shown, sexual symbols are more pronounced in Han popular discourse about ethnic Others in China, which is, however, informed and guided to a large extent by the official/state discourse.

## INTERNAL OTHERS IN CHINA

The representations of Internal Others in China thus exhibit the collusions or convergences of two streams: the official/state force and the force of the populace.

### The Official Discourse

A consensus in Western academia is that the hierarchical or patriarchal relationship between the Han and minority Others today has been inherited from the Qing and earlier Chinese empires.[9] This legacy is characterized by the notion that the Han were (and are) at the center of civilization while minorities were (and are) at the periphery. The Chinese empire had long ago endorsed a set of doctrines and practices that came to be characterized as "Chinese Culturalism" (Harrell 2001, 27). This is an ideology that sets Confucian ideals and political doctrines as the model of human civilization. The civility level of minorities and their relationship with the civilizing center were defined mostly in moral-cultural terms. Kinship and origin were not counted as the most important criteria, but the degrees to which minorities adopted Han cultural practices were measured on a scale of their "evolution" and assimilation. Some of them were very close to "civilized" Han or even verged on becoming Han.[10] Based on their civility level, other minorities were classified in two broad categories: "strange barbarians" (*sheng fan*) and "familiar barbarians" (*shu fan*).[11] The empire at the center launched a "civilizing project" to educate these minorities about the "proper rites" (*li*) and correct manners, and it measured their civility based on how much they accepted and absorbed these "high" cultural practices (Harrell 1995, 2001).

With the founding of the People's Republic of China in 1949, the Chinese Communist Party started to revise the empire-civilizing project to fit the socialist ideology of minorities and classes. Based on Marxist-Leninist theories of ethnic relations, the minority issue is understood as one form of class struggle, and social inequality was the soil and "nutrition" of minority difference. So the Party considered its most pressing task to be erasing the sources of such inequality, ultimately bringing minority groups to full and equal status with the Han. The Party also claims that such inequality will not easily disappear and will linger for a long time, but what the Party can do first of all is to grant minorities full political equality and equal rights to economic and cultural development. In this process, the Han have the obligation to help minorities advance together. According to Stevan Harrell (2001), the Party's civilizing project in China resembles neither an empire model nor a nation-state model. The empire model, characterized by the paradigm of the polarized center versus the periphery and superiority versus inferiority, was accused of being feudal and oppressive due to its legitimization of unequal relationships between the Han and minorities. As for the nation-state model, seeing that it intends to erase the cultural differences of minorities in order to promote a unified cultural system, the Party views this model as hegemonic and chauvinistic.

As a result, the Party promotes a new model that it refers to as "a unified country of diverse ethnicities" (*duo minzu de tongyi guojia*) or "a single unity with multiple cells" (*duoyuan yiti geju*), an expression coined by a leading Chinese sociologist-anthropologist, the late Fei Xiaotong (1910–2005), in 1989. The socialist model proposes that minority cultures are an integrative and indispensable part of the Zhonghua (the pan-Chinese nation including minorities) civilization and enjoy equal status with the Han culture. Nevertheless, in reality, what is promulgated as "a single unity" turns out to be "unified with or under the Han." Thus, the basic structure of the Han as the core with minorities on the periphery remains. Therefore, although the socialist model claims to be different from both the empire model and the nation-state model, it is actually a combination of the two— that is, the patronizing-patronized relationship between the Han and minorities still informs and shapes ethnic policies and ethnic interactions in China, while "a single unity with multiple cells" means that the minority Others must erase some, if not all, of their differences in order to fit into that unity with the "civilized" Han. In this way, the official discourse of ethnic Others has come into being.

From 1953 to 1957, the Chinese government organized a large-scale ethnic identification project.[12] This project and the Party's concept of ethnicity were informed by and embedded in the Morgan-Engels paradigm of social evolutionism: primitive society → slave society → feudalism → capitalism → socialism. Minorities were said to be on the lower rungs of the evolutionary ladder. Some ethnic groups were thought to be at the stage of primitive society, such as the Jinpo, Wa, Jinuo, Dulong, and Oroqen, among others. Many minority cultural practices were depicted as "primitive" and "backward," such as the "walking marriage" (*zouhun*) of the matrilineal Mosuo people (discussed below), and thus in need of reform. In Chinese official discourse, this custom is a remnant of the primitive "matrilineal clan" (*muxi shizu*), which is not congruent with socialist morality and ideals and thus must be eradicated.[13] Ironically, this "primitive" custom has now become an object of tourist fascination and source of revenue. The Party employed the evolutionary paradigm to legitimize its civilizing project of moralizing and "helping" minorities by changing their modes of production, lifestyles, and "outdated" customs, including "primitive" sexuality and even "mentality" (*sixiang guannian*), in order to accelerate their evolution. In this way, the Han act as fatherly figures or older brothers who will lead minorities in the construction of a socialist modernity.

However, the official discourse about minorities in China has been changing since then. In official propaganda, media, and textbooks today, there has been a growing tendency to incorporate Internal Others into the Chinese historical self through a new narrative that, in contrast to their portrayal as "foreigners" in the early 1950s, claims that they have always been Chinese (Baranovitch 2010, 85). As a result, not only the Han but also all minorities in China become "creators of history." This shift has to do with the Party's reflection on intensified ethnic conflicts in both international and domestic political arenas. Therefore, it is of strategic importance to define Tibet, Xinjiang, and other minority regions (as well as Taiwan) as "inseparable parts of China since antiquity [*ziguyilai*]" in textbooks, media, and other channels by refuting the separatists' claims. It is undeniable that the natural resources of minority regions, political stability, and support of state agendas by minorities are of great significance to China's economic and political success in the world. Thus, the state finds it beneficial to bring minorities' initiatives into play as well as to reassert China's sovereignty over minority regions and the legitimacy of extracting various resources. Some scholars have also argued that this change is inseparable from the growing influence of minority elites in challenging the Han-centric discourse (though not the unity of multicultural China) (Baranovitch 2010; see also Harrell and Li 2003).

### The Popular Discourse

Apart from the official discourse, there is also a popular discourse deeply grounded in mainstream Chinese society that informs the images of minorities and ethnic relations, which range from demonization to romanticization in the eyes of both elites who do not represent the state or officials and the common Han populace. The official discourse sets the framework for representations of minority groups, and, to a large extent, the popular discourse about minorities echoes the same theme of high (Han) culture versus low (minority) culture with the image of the Han as father or elder brother to minorities. As both discourses are embedded in each other, any attempt to separate them is doomed to fail. The popular discourse is characterized by the debasing of certain minorities as "wild," "dangerous," "barbarian," or "backward," on the one hand, and fascination and mystification of the "exotic" customs and cultures of minorities, on the other. Tibetans and Uyghurs have been denounced as ungrateful and treacherous largely as a result of the 2008 Tibet riot and 2009 Xinjiang upheaval. This negative labeling is the result of large-scale political propaganda about the nature of these rebellions, which describes them as separatist riots undertaken in collusion with vicious anti-China Western powers and diasporic cliques as well as violent incidents characterized by ruthless attacks on innocent civilians, governmental agencies, and other facilities. As this rhetoric invoked anti-Tibetan and anti-Uyghur sentiments, the whole Chinese nation, including minorities, united to condemn the violence of the rebels. Often such indignation among the general public was extended to innocent Tibetan and Uyghur people, who, as members of their ethnic groups, were also reviled and discredited.

On the whole, however, the popular discourse is overloaded with the exoticization of minority culture, and Others continue to be fetishized for their exoticness. According to Dru Gladney (1991, 1994) and Louisa Schein (1997, 2000), this is an exemplary manifestation of internal orientalism. A most prominent orientalist image is the portrayal of minorities as the embodiment of purity, simplicity, and unaffected optimism, while many urban Han people argue that they are lacking in such qualities because of the negative effects of modern life. In modern society, the common obsession with authenticity and traditions[14] typically reflects nostalgia for something that has been lost, and these "virtues" are often promoted as models for "corrupted," "desperate," and "civilized" Han that will allow them to lead authentic and meaningful lives.

Throughout Chinese history, some negative qualities normally associated with Others, such as wildness and savagery, have been praised and promoted as the remedy for the Han's deadly and morbid civility. In this way, some reform-minded individuals employ the "savagery" of Others as a critique of the "too civilized" Han. *Wolf Totem* is the best illustration of the Han's self-reflectivity in this respect, and the author's call for the Han to "go wild" by absorbing the wolfish nature of nomadic Mongols subverts dominant discourses about minorities and acknowledges the indispensable role of Internal Others in sustaining Chinese civilization. Once again, the Han construct selfhood as opposed to minorities but this time elevate minorities as masters and models for the Han to imitate. In so doing, this image of "noble Others" reverses the normative Han-self, which is culturally and morally superior to the "barbarian" Others.

Besides these two images of "authentic Others" and "noble Others," the image of "sexualized Others" is a common representation of Internal Others in China. In this portrayal, some minority men are recognized for their virility, toughness, and fearlessness—quintessential masculine properties that Han males are seen to lack and which they badly need in order to invigorate themselves.[15] This masculinized image of Others is consistent with the popular image of minority men, such as Tibetans and Mongolians, as hypermasculine or oversexed—well-built, courageous, rough, wild, and sexually potent. As a result, Other men become the object of both desire and fear for many Han men and women, in whose eyes Others qualify as "real men" for whom scholarly, "weak," urban Han men are no match. Other men could also be dangerous and unpredictable due to their unfettered wildness.

Likewise, minority women are often pictured as sexually open and promiscuous (Harrell 1995; Davis 2005). Some Han men complain that Han women are too rigid and "conservative" (*baoshou*) in sexual relationships, while the minority women of their imaginations are not confined by Confucian and traditional ideals and are more "open" (*kaifang*) and "free" (*ziyou*) in their selection of sexual partners. As a result, Other women became objects of sexual desire or of the male gaze. Propelled by this fantasy, many a male tourist goes to "the land of seductive women" to "have fun," and in some ethnic-tourist destinations, prostitution is booming.[16] Real minority women and Han women in ethnic costumes use their bodies to satisfy Han men's thirst for wild romance (Hyde 2001; Davis 2005, 10). The most popular image of free love in China is associated with the Mosuo people living by Lugu Lake.

## THE LURE OF LUGU LAKE:
### DISCOURSE OF THE WOMEN'S COUNTRY

Lugu Lake is located at the border between Yunnan and Sichuan in south-western China and is well known as the Women's Country throughout China. It is inhabited by the Mosuo, whose official status is contested.[17] The unique practice of walking marriage among the natives—a sexual partner-ship based on "romantic" love between a woman and her lover(s)—is highly popularized in China. The Han and other minority ethnic groups tend to react in two distinct ways to this practice. Many detest the "looseness" and "barbarism" of this custom, which seems completely at odds with the Confucian ideal of marriage and family and so-called universal standards practiced all over the world; many others are amazed by and envious of the free love at Lugu Lake, viewing it as an antithesis of or resistance to the rigid Chinese institution of marriage, which stifles people's sexuality and barely has any place for romance. Whatever the reaction, the practice at Lugu Lake is exotic to the Han and triggers their curiosity about the Women's Country. As a result, it has become a popular tourist destination and attracts tens of thousands of tourists each year, both from home and abroad.

Mosuo society is often advertised as "the last matriarchy on earth" or "the living fossil of matriarchy." Its walking-marriage practice fuels the imaginations of Han men, who imagine that Mosuo women can have relations with any man they like, that they just wait in their chambers for their lovers at night, and that they can also break up with and change their sexual partners at will. For some, the best part of it is that men are not obligated to take any responsibility for the possible consequences of their romantic love with these women, namely, children, who will be taken care of by their maternal families. This is believed to constitute the essence of free love. This myth appeals to an increasing number of Han and other male and some female tourists.[18] It also contributes to the popularization of the idea of the Women's Country all over China.

The reason Mosuo society is said to be a matriarchy has much to do with the fact that it is founded largely on matrilineal kinship: the children born out of the union of a woman and her partner(s) belong to the mother's lineage and are brought up by the immediate members of this lineage; the genitor doesn't normally participate in the economic life of this lineage. As mentioned above, the label of "matriarchy" is sanctioned by the official discourse stemming from the Morgan-Engels evolutionary pattern of human societies, and the popular discourse also takes it as such. The concept of the Women's Country is extremely popular with the Han and other minorities due to the unprecedented influence of the novel and adapted TV series *Journey to the West*, which is based on a legend about a Tang dynasty monk and his three disciples overcoming hardships as they travel all the way to Buddha's Land (India) to acquire holy scriptures. In one of their adventures, they set foot in the Women's Country, which is populated exclusively by women who become pregnant and give birth to female offspring by drinking from the Motherhood River. The Han and others can easily connect the Women's Country with Mosuo society.

In the popular imagination, the Women's Country or Mosuo society represents a number of features: (1) an abundance of good-looking women; (2) high female status, with women (usually elderly) taking the role of household head and women's opinions being more important in public affairs; (3) the popularity of female-centered local customs, such as the girls' puberty ritual and worship of the female mountain deity; (4) practices associated with women's freedom and control in matters of love, such as the ability to walk out of ordinary marriage and initiate as well as terminate sexual relationships; and, last but not least, (5) the predominance of cooperative, caring, and devoted relations among members of the extended family as well as in the whole community. In the eyes of many Han people, this utopian way of life contrasts with that of the Han at every point.[19]

## THE WOMEN'S COUNTRY—AN UNFULFILLED DREAM

A novel titled *The Remote Country of Women* (Yuanfang youge nüerguo), written in 1988 by the famous Chinese writer Bai Hua, is one of many works that have contributed to the creation, popularization, and essentialization of such images. As one of the most influential books on the Women's Country, this work distinguishes itself from most media products (movies, documentaries, travel brochures, books, blogs) on this "mysterious" land by being a serious reflection on and sharp critique of Han "civility" and mentality.[20] Like *Wolf Totem*, it juxtaposes the "sophisticated" Han with "innocent" minority people, namely the Mosuo, as a way of expressing the protagonist's, as well as the author's, frustration with the Han's shallowness, arrogance, and chauvinism. Mosuo society is portrayed as a paradise where people live a simple but happy life and celebrate and savor free love.

The main character, Liangrui, is swept up in the revolutionary tides of the 1960s and 1970s that undermined personal conscience and human nature. He shows no sympathy for his parents, who commit suicide at the beginning of the Cultural Revolution, declaring that their deaths are "as light as a feather." Appalled by the political chaos, he grows more and more disturbed by his own impassivity and cruelty. He becomes a pained but awakened observer of the craziness and consequences of endless political struggles: distrust, hypocrisy, hatred, mercilessness, violence, and betrayal. His life is overwhelmed by darkness, and he is unable to see any hope ahead. His only light is his girlfriend—the daughter of the former vice mayor—who provides a temporary refuge from the harsh and stifling reality. However, when her life returns to normal after the Cultural Revolution, their relationship comes to an end. Liangrui decides to leave his sufferings and urban life behind and work in a faraway land. His accidental encounter with two hospitable Tibetan girls when he arrives at his destination convinces him that he has come to a place where the people are simple and pure of heart.

The other thread in *The Remote Country of Women* is the story of Sunamei, a beautiful and innocent Mosuo girl who has grown up in a totally different environment where people are sincere, caring, warm, trustworthy, lighthearted, free-spirited, and good-natured. In her harmonious society, there is no murder for love, conflict between in-laws, family discord over money or power, or abandonment of the elderly and orphans, and women are free to love or not to love and, above all, are the soul of society. They are diligent in work, dedicated to their families, and capable of managing a big household. However, their most distinctive quality is that they love just for the sake of love without considering external factors such as wealth, "morality," or family pressure. Therefore, Mosuo men are the luckiest men in the world because their lovers devote their whole hearts to them. Likewise, Mosuo women are the most blessed because the Mosuo men here are unusually understanding and broad-minded, never starting fights or making trouble if their women find new loves. Since this culture doesn't keep a rein on people's hearts and allows them natural expression, Sunamei's life is full of joys. Her lovers treat her as a priceless gem, and she enjoys passionate moments of physical and emotional unity with them. However, her life is transformed when she is selected to work in the county's performance troupe due to her extraordinary singing talent.

The two threads converge when the disillusioned former revolutionary youth and passionate and "wild" Sunamei—two people from totally different worlds—meet at the county theater where Liangrui works and Sunamei performs. They fall in love and live together in secret. She is lonely and homesick in the county seat where people (Han) are afraid of expressing love in either words or actions. She is watched and guarded against all the time because of the assumed promiscuous and unbridled nature of Mosuo women. The women in town are worried that she will slip into their houses at night to sleep with their husbands. She becomes a target of gossip. Liangrui is also concerned about her "wildness" and hopes to use marriage to curb her unruliness. As he wishes, she turns into an obedient "small wife" (*xiaoxifu*), and he assumes that she belongs to him only. This dream is shattered when they go to her natal home and she and her ex-lover are caught cheating on him. In a fury, he beats her and causes a big fire. She disappears, and he realizes that he will never belong to this world and so must return to the world he has tried to escape.

Unlike most Han, Liangrui thinks highly of Mosuo culture, including walking marriage, and asserts that Mosuo society has a higher moral standard than the Han's, thanks to their unfettered passion for life and the ability to be true to their own hearts. In spite of this, he attempts to subjugate his "wild" Mosuo wife and educate her with the ethics of "modern" marriage. His failure is manifested not only in his marriage but also in his life more broadly, when he ends up being unable to belong to either the Other world or the "civilized" modern world. The word "remote" in the book's title doesn't simply refer to geographic distance but reflects psychological distance and a cultural gap that make the remote land even more alluring.

Bai Hua's work essentializes and idolizes Mosuo culture and practices, especially free love, catering to and enhancing the Han's craving for this mysterious and faraway land. His reflections on Han sophistication and chauvinism also reinforce the image of "innocent," "carefree," and "sensual" Mosuo people, especially the women. The protagonist represents merely one of millions of Han tourists and others who travel to Lugu Lake with extravagant yearnings.

## Being Real for Tourists

The utopian way of life at Lugu Lake and especially such "exotic" customs as walking marriage have great appeal for Han tourists who flock to Lugu Lake to explore or experience this unusual tradition. Many of them are eager to find out how many partners locals have and how they form such relationships. In 2004, when I first visited this lake, a local woman told me that tourists always liked to ask these private questions, which embarrassed or even irritated her a lot at first, but she eventually got used to it. In fact, many locals engage in "auto-orientalism" in order to cater to the curiosity and desires of tourists (see Blumenfield 2010). For instance, some Mosuo people joke with inquisitive tourists about their so-called free-love practices and tease them about "tasting" local women or men. Many Mosuo counteract the negative effect of their reputation for free love or promiscuity by emphasizing their loving and harmonious family structure in front of visitors (Walsh 2005).

Nevertheless, locals know that the free-love myth is the part of their culture that attracts tourists' interest and money. Yang Erche Namu, a highly controversial female celebrity in China, a writer and former singer originally from Lugu Lake, plays an important role in promoting the image of Mosuo as carefree lovers. Yang's portrayal of the innocent and sexually "instinctual" Mosuo is so influential that several minority members told me that Yang was causing not only Mosuo but all minorities to lose face. To quote one Tibetan woman, "Yang Erche Namu must be out of her mind. What is she doing? She created the image that we minorities are *luan gao* [having chaotic sexual intercourse]" (*luan* means "chaotic," and *gao* means "doing," "making," or, in this case, "sexual intercourse"). Yang Erche Namu's self-orientalizing and sexualizing of the Mosuo have also been mentioned by critics of her coauthored English-language autobiography *Leaving Mother Lake* (Yang Erche Namu and Mathieu 2003).

Lugu Lake is thus imagined by many Han and others as a land for romantic encounters, where one can leave behind all one's sexual constraints and live purely for love—at least for one amorous night. It happens that some local women and men may want to "taste" outsiders, too, but surely such impulses are not enough to meet the demands of the tourist market. As a result, prostitution appeared and returns from time to time in spite of governmental crackdowns. The sex workers, mostly non-Mosuo from other poor regions, all wear Mosuo costumes and satisfy the desires of guests who seek free love with "authentic" Mosuo women, even though it is obvious that this love is not free (Walsh 2005).

The matriarchy discourse plays into such essentialized erotic scripts, and escalating tourism revenues have spurred further commercialization of the Women's Country and local traditions (see Blumenfield 2010). Drawing from Lugu Lake's successful experience, Danba County in Sichuan and some other places also hope to promote their versions of the Women's Country.

In the tourist markets of China, the Eastern Queendom is well known, too. Like the Women's Country at Lugu Lake, Danba is also advertised by the local government and media as the land of beautiful women who are higher in status than men and engage in romantic love at will. This advertisement has contributed to the inflow of tens of thousands of tourists each year, many of whom are fascinated with this myth. Therefore, the popularity of the matriarchy discourse emanates at least in part from the market value of the sexually charged label "Women's Country," which is, however, deeply rooted in the official and popular discourse about minority women and men.

Although women in the Women's Country tend to be depicted as "feminine" or "gentle and soft" (*wenrou*), Yang Erche Namu is notorious for her wildness and bluntness. The most common comments I heard from people, both the Han and minorities, are that she is "crazy," "thick-skinned," and "unashamed." She is inclined to make audacious remarks to the media. For instance, her proposal of marriage to French president Nicolas Sarkozy during his visit to China in 2007 became sensational news in China and abroad. She has labeled herself "the biggest bitch in China." Since Yang often speaks as if she were the spokesperson for all minorities, her self-portrayal reaffirms the image of "unruly" minority people in the Han popular discourse in China. A popular myth even credits Miao women with poisoning outsiders by magic (see Diamond 1988; Harrell 1995; Schein 2000). Nevertheless, the "wild" nature of minority women may make them even more attractive to Han men, who see their own ability to tame the former's wildness as a public declaration of their heroism and virility.

*Wolf Totem* and the discourse on the Women's Country help illustrate how minorities are represented in both the popular and the official discourse in China. In the popular discourse, minorities are often sexualized, normally portrayed as either hypermasculine or hyperfeminine. These images are shaped and structured by the official discourse, which is dominated by Han-minority patronization. Although minorities sometimes become symbolically central in the Han endeavor to rediscover themselves through Internal Others, this doesn't necessarily bring about due respect or even liberation for minorities. Minority images, whether feminized or masculinized, positive or negative, are often appropriated by the state and the Han for their own consumption and nationalist self-absorption.

This is mostly a one-sided fantasy. The voices and self-expressed interests of Others are often not of concern; thus, minority people's intentions and opinions can be brushed aside and their identities defined and interpreted through the lens of the Han or the state. In this context, the Suopowa's struggle for the queendom label is of particular significance.

## Chapter 3

# FROM THE VALLEY OF BEAUTIES
# TO THE EASTERN QUEENDOM

✳

Due to its breathtaking landscape, exquisite Tibetan-style buildings, and unique customs, the media promote Danba as the Most Beautiful Countryside in China ( Zhongguo Zui Meili de Xiangcun). However, Danba's popularity among tourists has much to do with its fame as the Valley of Beauties (Meirengu). The media and tourists undeniably have played an essential role, but the local state, elites, and villagers have also actively participated in the process of forging the Valley of Beauties and the Eastern Queendom. Their involvement raises many questions: Are locals conscious of the negative or sexualized connotations of popular labels? How do their responses speak to the complex terrain of ethnic representations in China? How can we make sense of the competition over the Eastern Queendom brand and the brand's coexistence with "authentic" Khampa hypermasculinity? More specifically, why do Suopo men choose to feminize themselves in order to cater to the Han's or tourists' fantasies? Are they doing so because they intend to reverse the dominant power structure, or is their choice subject to more nuanced macroscopic and microscopic conditions that define them as more than potential "insurgents"? The making of the queendom and the Valley of Beauties is largely in the hands of men. If women are superior to men, as Suopo male elites claim, why are women not more active in the queendom project?

FIG. 3.1. Gyarong Charm Festival, Danba, 2009. Photo courtesy of the Danba Culture and Tourism Bureau

## MAKING THE VALLEY OF BEAUTIES

The media's successful promotion of the "Valley of Beauties" label since 2001 has brought an increasing number of tourists to Danba each year. An important agenda for many tourists is seeing (and perhaps embracing) good-looking Danba women. The local government has been working closely with the media to enhance Danba's status as the land of beauties in the Chinese tourist market. Danba County has organized five Gyarong Charm Festivals (Jiarong Fengqingjie) since 2001 (see fig. 3.1) and invited TV stations, newspapers, and magazines to these events.

The most popular component of this festival is the beauty contest. Dozens of beautiful young women from all over Danba, wearing elegant clothing and magnificent jewels, gather at the county seat for this competition (see fig. 3.2). The winners are granted three levels of prizes: Golden Flower is first prize, Silver Flower is second prize, and Guava Flower is third prize.[1] Journalists from important media are often invited to serve as judges. As a result, elaborate reports on and numerous photos of graceful and glamorous

FIG. 3.2. Beauty pageant contestants, 2009. Photo courtesy of the Danba Culture and Tourism Bureau

Danba women are spread all over China, especially on the Internet. This practice has contributed greatly to the soaring reputation of Danba as the Valley of Beauties.

An ironic consequence of the escalating regard for Danba beauties in China is that a lot of tourists complain that they don't see very many beautiful women in Danba. Sometimes, locals respond that the beauties have all gone to big cities for jobs, leaving behind their mothers and grandmothers for the tourists' gaze. Hundreds of young Danba women have in fact been hired by singing and dancing troupes or companies in tourist attractions all over China and in such big cities as Chengdu, Beijing, Shanghai, and Guangzhou.

Many locals take pride in the "Valley of Beauties" label. They often authenticate and defend Danba's claim to fame in front of tourists. I have often heard local guides and others introduce courtship customs and free-love practices in Danba to tourists. In this way, locals cater to tourists' fascination with the "authentic" and "romantic" local traditions of the Valley of Beauties.

## RESPONSES TO THE SEXUALIZED IMAGE
## OF WOMEN IN THE VALLEY OF BEAUTIES

Are locals aware that some tourists come to the Valley of Beauties not just for a glimpse of beautiful local women or to hear stories of "exotic" customs but for free love or romantic encounters with Danba women? During an early stage of tourism development at the turn of this century, many locals didn't realize that local women would become sexual objects for male tourists, but in the past several years in Jiaju, Suopo, and other parts of Danba, people often reminded me that some tourists had "other thoughts" when they came to Danba because of their fascination with the name "Valley of Beauties" or "Eastern Queendom." Some local people expressed concern about possible "degeneration" among the youth, especially girls, who participated in the tourism industry as local guides or receptionists, and about the corruption of local culture and traditions. In tourist-frequented villages such as Jiaju—best known for its magnificent architecture and landscape (see fig. 3.3), which attracts the largest number of tourists who visit Danba— there were often rumors among villagers that some girls had sexual relations with tourists. As one Jiaju man in his late fifties commented, "Now society has changed. The girls [in the village] used to feel very shy when they saw strangers. Today only the 'shameless' girls can make money. They would do anything for tourists for the sake of money. Sometimes two girls would be fighting with each other for a wealthy [male] tourist. Many elderly villagers say that these 'thick-skinned' girls have made all our Jiaju [people] lose face completely."

I knew an unmarried female guide from Jiaju in her early twenties who was often designated by county governmental agencies to be a guide for guests such as visiting officials and journalists due to her excellent standard Chinese (Mandarin), eloquence, and elegance. She was later offered a temporary position as a "receptionist" at the county's Reception Office, which received and entertained visiting VIPs and other guests of the county government and Communist Party committee. After one or two weeks at work, she returned home for a short break and was dumbfounded when her father asked, "Have you slept with someone?" although she knew that many villagers thought that the Reception Office was staffed by handsome young men and especially beautiful women who were good at speaking and drink-

FIG. 3.3. Jiaju is promoted as the Most Beautiful Village in China. Owners repaint their distinctively styled houses every year based on tradition and/or in return for a portion of the county's tourism revenue. Photo courtesy of the Danba Culture and Tourism Bureau

ing and might try every means to entertain guests, including sex. According to one villager, because of her job, some villagers labeled this girl a "Tibetan whore." Local female guides and other "flirtatious" girls who interacted with male tourists in an "overly friendly" manner were also portrayed in this way. Such labeling expresses the accumulated anxiety among villagers over the negative effect of tourism on local society, in which a money-driven mentality has disrupted traditional values including self-dignity and sexual norms for women.

"Sexually open" Jiaju girls are often blamed for having sexual relations with tourists, while some locals claim that tourism and the Han, or abstract agents such as social change or money, have contributed in general to sexual exchange or moral decay. According to one high school teacher,

> In the past, [local] people lived a good life without much money. Now there is more money, and tourists also come. There are all kind of tourists—some are good, some are bad, and some just come here to look for women. They have destroyed everything. Now society develops, [but local] people

are not happy anymore. Some women rely on their [beautiful] faces to make a living. . . . These are all caused by money.

Another view, represented by an elite man from Suopo, blames the Han and tourists as well as locals.

Many Han [men] came here just for women. They even asked me where they could find beautiful women for the night. What are they thinking about? They think they can do everything they want because they have money. We minority people have our dignity. But to tell you the truth, sometimes I don't know what to say. Some [local] people don't [have dignity]. They do everything possible for the sake of money. Even people from Jiaju are talking about their women. They [Jiaju women] don't know what they are doing. We Zangzu have precious traditions. What has happened? Some people [Zangzu] are even worse than the Han. I don't even want to talk about it [*sighs*].

This man was upset about the condescending attitude of Han tourists who believe in the power of money and impose a "dirty image" on local Zangzu women. He was also annoyed by "shameless" local people who exchange their dignity or bodies for money. In his view, Zangzu generally have higher moral standards than Han, who are believed to have no religion and thus lack restraint. However, because of the influence of tourists and "bad" Han culture, some locals have changed and become Sinicized. Therefore, the blame belongs both to the Han and tourists who have brought influences such as prostitution and to locals who cannot resist the temptation of immoral earnings.

To this elite Suopo man, "loose" Jiaju women are an object of ridicule and condemnation. I often heard some Suopo villagers accuse certain Jiaju women of being "promiscuous" and "selling their bodies." To quote one woman from Moluo, in Suopo Township,

While I was selling apples [to tourists] at the viewpoint platform [*guanjingtai*; a platform by the highway across the Dadu River from which to view the stone watchtowers in Moluo and several other villages in Suopo], I saw a bus come to a stop, and a [female] guide from Jiaju got off, followed by a group of tourists. A woman at the end of this group said to another one, "Tibetan whore" [*zangmao*; lit., "Tibetan cat"], pointing to this Jiaju guide who stood at the edge of the platform far away. I didn't know what she was referring to. I thought there was a cat somewhere, so I looked around but didn't see any. Then another young girl from my village told me that she didn't mean "cat," and she was talking about "prostitute." . . . I heard later that many Jiaju girls did such a thing with [male] tourists. What a shame! We Suopowa can never do it.

Two important messages are conveyed here: first, some locals have become conscious of the sexualized image of local women among tourists as their interactions increase; and second, condemning "loose" Jiaju girls delineates a boundary between "pure us" and "impure them." This negative attitude toward Jiaju women (and the money-loving Jiajuwa in general) was not uncommon among Suopo villagers. A direct reason for the general negative impression of Jiaju in Suopo is that many a person from Suopo has not been happy about the Jiajuwa's success in the tourist market. Many Suopo villagers blame the Jiajuwa for sullying Suopo's reputation by telling tourists that Suopo is "dirty," that there is "nothing" to see over there, that it is a "nest of tuberculosis," and that the Suopowa "always cheat tourists." In reproaching the Jiajuwa for decadence and corruption, the Suopowa oppose these insults and assert their own moral superiority. In their portrayal, Suopo villagers have held onto the authentic Tibetan identity, while Jiaju has been "polluted" by money and the "bad culture" of the Han. Suopo women are said to be morally superior to and better than Jiaju women because they uphold ancient tradition, which Suopo's queendom advocates will assert is the queendom tradition that is centered on women's prestige and dignity.

Therefore, although the Suopowa's embrace of the "Eastern Queendom" label can be easily read as an indigenous marketing plan in the tourist market, it is at the same time a conscious retrieval of their portrayal from the sexualized image and negative connotation of the Valley of Beauties. It also marks an ethical boundary that differentiates them from the "disreputable" Jiajuwa. Thus, what the Suopowa are stressing in the queendom discourse is not physical beauty but women's political wisdom and dignity—a conscious shying away from the Valley of Beauties discourse in favor of the Eastern Queendom discourse of women's authority.

## "SUPERIOR" WOMEN, BUT THE MEN'S QUEENDOM

A popular explanation for the charm of women from Danba is that their noble blood is responsible for their unusual elegance and gracefulness, since they descend from the Xixia king and nobles, some of whose immediate family members managed to flee to Danba and neighboring places when their kingdom was destroyed by Mongol troops in 1227 (see, e.g., Xueniu 2003; Yang and Yang 2004).[2] This story explains the abundance of beauties in Danba as well as the label "Valley of Beauties." In 2001, Danba County even sent several beautiful local women to pay a visit to their "ancestors" in Ningxia Hui Autonomous Region in northwest China, which attracted much attention from the media and the public (Wu 2001). Another common explanation is based on local connections with the Eastern Queendom (see also Xueniu 2003; Yang and Yang 2004). Local people are said to carry noble blood from the elegant queens. Danba locals, especially tour guides, often call upon these beliefs to explain the abundance of beauties in the Valley of Beauties. Nevertheless, the Suopowa's queendom discourse is very different from these two claims in that it focuses on women's status in sociopolitical life in Suopo rather than on royal blood.

To be more specific, Uncle Pema and other Suopo queendom advocates have been cognizant of the negative implication of the labels attached to the Valley of Beauties and the Eastern Queendom. Although they claim that Suopo women are elegant and beautiful, they argue that this does not make local women special but that it is their esteemed status and natural leadership that render them extraordinary. These Suopo elite men routinely mention what a glory it was for the Suopowa that three local women village leaders were sent to Beijing and received by Chairman Mao in the 1950s and 1960s. But if local women are more politically sophisticated, why are all the principal queendom advocates men? How did this men's queendom come about?

A simple answer is that the supposed superior status of women in Suopo's sociopolitical life is manipulated by local men for tourists and outsiders. Women's inconspicuous and indirect involvement in the queendom dispute is consistent with the low profile of women in local political matters in general, such as elections. At present, not one woman holds an important position in any of the eleven villages in Suopo Township. According to the two former women heads of Moluo Village who were sent to Beijing to see

Mao, most of the young men were dispatched to various positions outside the village in the 1950s and 1960s, and thus women were obliged to do men's work, such as plowing the land and taking important positions that they had not sought. One was promoted to the village leadership because of her husband's position in the People's Liberation Army (PLA). As the wife of a "glorious" PLA officer, she proved her qualifications and loyalty to the Party but had to demonstrate her "redness" by taking more demanding jobs, like being village head. The other former village head indicated that she hadn't wanted to be a Party member because she had no idea what it entailed, and she hadn't aspired to village leadership because it required her to take on many more responsibilities. Due to her "red" class background of coming from a poor family and her diligence at work, she was promoted as a Party member first and then became the village head against her wishes. Although both of them demonstrated their excellent organizational skills and leadership by establishing Moluo Village as the Model Village throughout Danba County, it was not the so-called queendom tradition of valuing women over men that had put them into such positions. Moluo women's leadership and prominent role were instead a political product of a time and circumstance when eligible men were not present.

When that era was over, men returned and started to take over most of the important positions. In 1998, the last woman village head, who was well recognized for her uprightness, fairness, and working capacities, died of cancer, and since then, no woman has taken a village leadership position. Today, women's traditional roles as wives and mothers remain intact despite signs of positive change.[3] Men dominate the political and nondomestic spheres in Suopo and Danba, and women are not actively involved in political matters.

When I asked Suopo women for their views on the queendom dispute, many expressed a negative attitude toward Zhonglu "thieves" and the complicity of county cadres. Nonetheless, very few were enthusiastic advocates for the queendom cause. They attributed their lack of involvement to low literacy, lack of skill at public speaking in standard Chinese, and preoccupation with farmwork and housework. A consensus is that the queendom dispute is a public matter that involves intensive negotiations with outsiders—township and county cadres, the media, and interested scholars or tourists. Since most women received little education, they are not confident about their negotiating and speaking skills, especially when the language used is Chinese. Most of them also claim that men have more time for political matters like the queendom struggle, while women have to take care of most of the household chores. It is interesting to note that many men expressed the same opinion on women's "indifference" toward this dispute.

At another level, theories of gender symbolism and hierarchy may shed light on Suopo men's enthusiasm for "their" queendom. As previously outlined, the powerful, such as colonial authorities and the political apparatuses they represent, may feminize Others by polarizing their normative notion of masculinity against subordinates' femininity as a way of justifying their own advantaged standing.[4] Surprisingly, however, men in a marginalized group may apply the feminizing strategy to their women as well (Schein 1997). Why do they do so? One theory is that the dominant party has inculcated the less privileged group with the ideology of the "proper order" of the world, so that the latter simply copies, repeats, and maintains the order established by the former (see, e.g., Bourdieu 1977). The other theory is that the less privileged people, males in this case, are able to circumvent the ruling party's control by empowering themselves through objectifying "their women" and commercializing their own ethnicity and traditions (Schein 1997; Oakes 1998). This latter theory doesn't deny the constraints of the structure but argues that the less powerful can find ways to get around them.

The Suopowa's struggle for their queendom cause exemplifies the second interpretation. The men gain both economic and symbolic capital and assert their identities by selling Suopo women's "superior" status and "political wisdom" to the media and tourists while simultaneously reminding them that good appearance does not constitute the essence of their Eastern Queendom agenda. Thus, the Suopowa's queendom discourse is a challenge to the superficial popular discourse of the Valley of Beauties that has put so much emphasis on good looks and sexualized images of Danba women while ignoring the women's important role in family and society.

## WHY SELF-FEMINIZATION?

As has been said, the Suopowa's queendom discourse attaches great importance to the significant status and unparalleled prestige of women in Suopo society. However, locals are engaged in more than promoting the political wisdom and high esteem of local women to the outside world: they are simultaneously feminizing themselves through propaganda exalting women's ingenuity and superiority vis-à-vis men throughout history. What complicates the picture is that they take pride in their masculinity at the same time. How can one make sense of this paradox?

The Suopowa speak a dialect close to the Kham Tibetan dialect, and this is cited as evidence of their status as "authentic" Khampa people whose culture is popularly characterized by virility among Tibetans and the Han. Some Suopo villagers I have encountered have a sense of superiority in comparison to other Gyarongwa, expressed by remarks such as "You Gyarongwa . . ." that declare their difference from other Gyarongwa. But if they are proud of their Kham lineage and masculinity, why don't they promote masculinity to the media and tourists as other Kham regions do? A practical reason may be that the assumed "women's culture" has been a part of traditions and customs as well as folktales and legends, and it is more convenient for them to embark on the queendom project.

Their claimed masculinity, however, is not well recognized by other Khampa people and the Han. Although they (and sometimes other Gyarongwa in Danba as well) are referred to as "Khampa" by the local state, the media, and tourists, they are marginalized Khampa, since other "authentic" Khampa do not accept them as equals. According to Suopo villagers who took odd jobs in other Khampa counties in Ganzi Tibetan Autonomous Prefecture, they were sometimes referred to as "fake Tibetans" or, even worse, "Han." Many villagers claim that they are Gyarongwa, so even if some Suopowa want to promote Khampa masculinity on a large scale, they may have difficulty obtaining enough support from within. Therefore, the Suopowa are at a disadvantage in competing in the tourist market for the authentic virility label with a broad area of Khampa regions in Sichuan, Yunnan, Qinghai, and the Tibet Autonomous Region. The feminine queendom model is much more viable and touristically appealing.

To some extent, self-feminization can be a strategy for seeking rewards from the powerful, including alleviated surveillance and loosened control. It may even serve as a challenge to the dominant structure. For instance, according to Mrinalini Sinha, Bengali elites' acceptance of the feminine image imposed by British colonists was not nonstrategic or passive, as it seemed to be:

On the one hand . . . the self-perception of effeminacy was itself an expression of the hegemonic aspiration of the Bengali elite: for the degeneration of the body of the elite Hindu male became the symbol of the negative impact of colonial rule on indigenous society as a whole. On the other hand, the self-perception of effeminacy also facilitated a challenge, however limited and contradictory, to the dominance of the colonizing elites: for the emasculation of Indians was also the basis for challenging specific colonial policies. (1995, 7)

The self-feminization of Bengali elites thus transformed the negative image of feminization into a critique of colonial policies and resistance to hegemonic colonial masculinity. The Suopowa's self-feminization may also be a challenge to the dominant structure and a strategy that accentuates the Suopowa's moral superiority. The queendom discourse about the superior status of women in Suopo is a public declaration that Suopo men value and respect women to an extent that men in other societies are unable to do. Suopo elites and villagers often express shock at the misogyny and low status of women in other Tibetan societies and among the Han. Suopo males thus know how to treat women "properly" and are morally superior to other Tibetans, the Han, and even Westerners. As real men, they are more masculine than all other men. As they highlight women's political wisdom and capacities rather than physical beauty, they emphasize the humanistic or gentlemanly aspect of masculinity instead of physical strength.

Suopo's elevation of women's status reflects the influence of the socialist gender-equality ideology of the Chinese state. A standard interpretation of women's status before Liberation in 1949 was that women were largely "owned" and treated as "property" by their families and thus were merely sacrificed to the feudal system. In seeking to revolutionize the new China and eradicate the residues of feudalism, the liberation of women from the tyranny of the outdated patriarchal system was an important task for the Party. Therefore, granting women equal status with men by law was at the top of the new government's agenda. The first Marriage Law of China, enacted in 1950, states that women have the freedom to marry or divorce and enjoy equal rights in all aspects of family and sociopolitical life. If women were to achieve this goal, the first step was to enter the public sphere that has been dominated by men (He 2008). The logic behind this statement is that women should take the same jobs as men and work as hard as men in order to prove their equality. As a result, femininity and womanhood were rejected. This view was developed to the fullest during the Cultural

Revolution, when "the Iron Girls—strong, robust, muscular women who boldly performed physically demanding jobs traditionally done by men"— became a model for millions of women in China, including minority women (Honig 2002, 55).

Suopo women, too, took important positions and played a significant role in political life between the 1950s and 1970s. The two women leaders of Moluo Village who were sent to Beijing to see Mao and several other women in their seventies and eighties all mentioned that they had to work as hard as they could for the commune—like men—and gender was not considered an excuse for any dereliction of duty. The socialist sexual-equality ideology had a great impact on the Suopowa's lives as it did in every part of China. It was not merely the temporary absence of men that caused women to be promoted as village heads; their elevation had everything to do with Maoist egalitarian ideology.

All the major queendom advocates were born in the 1950s and had intensive experience with political propaganda. Since the Cultural Revolution, the concept of gender equality has resounded in Suopo and all over China. Women's rights in politics, education, employment, and property ownership, as well as their rights as free individuals, are promulgated through official documents, the media, and schools. Almost all Suopowa are conscious of this "basic national policy" (*jiben guoce*) of China.

Although the notion of gender equality informs the Suopowa's queendom discourse, Suopo elites went further by proclaiming the superiority of Suopo women. They did this both to be consistent with the popular image of a queendom where women are absolute rulers and men are their subordinates and to appeal to tourists. Suopo males have also earned symbolic capital in so doing—their masculinity is not weakened but is, on the contrary, reaffirmed and strengthened.

In China's ethnic landscape and tourism market, Danba people, including the Suopowa, are sexualized or feminized, as are many other minorities. This representation situates locals in an inferior position, which constrains their choices and neglects their concerns. However, it also sets in motion their own initiatives in reinterpreting cultural traditions and expressing their modernist pursuits as agents of local social development and political reconfiguration. As is showcased in Danba and more specifically in Suopo, although the labels "Valley of Beauties" and "Eastern Queendom" have negative connotations, they have enhanced the locals' sense of pride and identity construction as well. In interactions with tourists, many Danba people have come to recognize the negative effect of sexualized images of Danba, and some, like the Suopo queendom advocates, have presented an alternative discourse that gives prominence to women's unmatched intelligence and prestige as well as their moral superiority to others, including the Han. The Suopowa's queendom discourse highlights local agency in their efforts to define "who we are" rather than being defined as "who they are" by the Han or the state. Although it does play a part in challenging the asymmetrical power structure between the Han and minorities and between tourists and locals, it is fair to say that this alternative discourse is often a response to specific state, Han, and tourist agendas rather than constituting full-scale resistance against the dominant structure or the state. As is demonstrated in the way that the Suopowa discredit the Jiajuwa in delineating the boundary and declaring their superiority, different segments or individuals in a given minority group may find scapegoats by stigmatizing others for the negative effects of such a structure and unbalanced power.

# Chapter 4

## THE QUEENDOM AND

## GRASSROOTS POLITICS

✳

Despite differing approaches to grassroots politics, many China scholars argue that intensified reforms in China have resulted in accumulating tensions in the countryside and that peasants have responded by acting collectively in protests, sit-ins, demonstrations, and petitions and also by using legal means of expressing their frustration and dissatisfaction with the state.[1] Rural agitators are usually "conscious of central government rules and adept at seizing on official rhetoric to press their claims" (O'Brien 2002, 146). In this way, they often situate themselves as supporters and defenders of central state agendas rather than as opponents and insurgents, seeking to legitimize their political claims in the hope that higher authorities and preferably even the central government will hear them and eventually address their grievances.

In the field, I was often surprised by the villagers' knowledge of the central government's political principles, such as "preferential policies for peasants" (*huinong zhengce*), including tax exemption and rural democratization. I was surprised because many of these mountain-dwelling Zangzu villagers were illiterate and could barely speak Chinese. How did they gain access to such knowledge?[2] Demonstrations, sit-ins, and "group appeals to higher authority" (*jiti shangfang*) have also increased sharply since 2005. These

concern mostly disputes over mining, such as damage to houses and dese-
cration of holy mountains, as well as protests over the expropriation of land
and the unequal compensation provided by governmental agencies and
state-owned or private corporations for their development programs,
mainly hydroelectric power projects.

Toward the end of 2008, a little more than half a year after the Tibetan
riots, the demonstrations resumed and even intensified. A township cadre
expressed consternation, saying of the villagers who went to a sit-in at the
county hall in May 2009, all of whom were women, "I don't know where
these illiterate people learned this 'trick.' Some of them may have never been
to the county seat before." Local Zangzu not only have learned to use protest
to voice their opinions but also have mastered it surprisingly well. The strategy of having only women demonstrators is based on the assumption that
the government and police wouldn't dare to treat them roughly due to the
general public's natural sympathy toward this "weak" group.

Why were local Zangzu villagers engaged in collective action? It became
clear to me that their opposition had little to do with independence, as
many outsiders or Tibet-cause advocates or sympathizers in the West and
other parts of the world imagine. Instead, they were fighting for their rights
as peasants and citizens in a mountainous region of China; they shared
the same concerns as their Han counterparts throughout China and
applied the same tactic of using "the regime's own words as a weapon" with
which to safeguard their "lawful rights and interests" (*hefa quanyi*) (O'Brien
2002, 147).

It was apparent that cadres and villagers in Danba distrusted each other.
Cadres sometimes called villagers "rogue civilians" (*diaomin*), while villagers accused cadres of being lazy, selfish, irresponsible, corrupt, and bureaucratic. Several Suopo Township cadres claimed that Suopo villagers were
the "wildest" in Danba County because they dared to challenge the cadres'
authority face-to-face, drove the township Party secretary into the river,
vandalized a gold mine, and demonstrated against the government at the
county seat. I also observed the frustration, anxiety, and conflict Suopo
villagers experienced in their daily lives and in pervasive disputes within
and among villages over elections, the distribution of social welfare, and
rights to the land, water, trees, stone watchtowers, and gold mines, as well
as in their interactions with township and county cadres.

Although cadres and villagers specify different reasons for their mutual dislike, they agree on one point, which is that the policies of the central government are very good, since both have benefited a great deal from expanding development projects in this Zangzu region.[3] At first, this statement perplexed me. If state or Party policies are very good, why is there tension between cadres and villagers? Some cadres argue that villagers are "spoiled" by the central state's preferential policies, while villagers grumble about the good things from above that go bad on the way down because the local state is tainted by "vice." I came to realize that villagers are negotiating their own identities as members of a specific village, segment,[4] and township, as Zangzu or Han and also as residents of Suopo Township and Danba County, and, finally, as Chinese citizens. Therefore, their dissatisfaction and frustration with local cadres is neither simply the amplification of their struggle at the grassroots level for their proper niche in the social and political structure of Danba nor only a struggle to reclaim the touristically lucrative "queendom" label. It is also the crystallization of internal and external differentiation and boundaries along the lines of locality, historical connections, culture and traditions, ethnic difference, and legal rights as Chinese citizens.

Suopo villagers declare that they are largely marginalized in Danba, based on their assumption that the county government has not attached enough importance to them. Many attribute this neglect to the fact that there are no native officials "at the court," namely, in county or higher-level governmental agencies. Villagers are most upset at present about the Suopo Bridge and the queendom issue. The bridge controversy has built up considerable tension and hostility since 2004.[5] The queendom dispute exacerbated this situation and is the issue most frequently brought up by the Suopowa as proof of their marginalized status in Danba. Many villagers express their contempt for the county for displaying favoritism on this issue. It is believed that Danba's preference of Zhonglu Township over Suopo as the supposed site for the ancient queens' palace has to do with the influence of Zhonglu native officials "at the court." Villagers vehemently curse these officials, and many swear that they will take extreme actions whenever necessary to force the county to back down.

Extreme actions are defined by the state as demonstrations of any kind, including "violent" acts against government agencies, public places, and innocent civilians. Also condemned under this label are group appeals to higher authority without local governmental approval. In response to such actions, the Chinese government has adopted a hard-line policy toward its Zangzu subjects by increasing the presence of the army as well as intensifying political surveillance and propaganda in all Zangzu regions, including Danba. Nonetheless, in the past five years, demonstrations have escalated in scale and number in Danba. Faced with defiant public denunciations of local officials, the county government has threatened to label the participants "insurgents" who are working against the Party's "stability maintenance" (weiwen) policy, the first and foremost principle in Tibetan regions since the riots. Suopo villagers say they may resort to even more extreme actions for their queendom cause if the government continues to ignore their petition to reclaim the queendom; however, they recognize the need for caution since the endless propaganda about the "Tibetan situation" on TV and from cadres has reminded them that this may not be the best time for them to take action. If the queendom dispute were labeled a political riot, all their efforts would be rendered meaningless.

The queendom dispute has thus become a symbolic stage on which the Suopowa stand up against the "vicious" local authorities to redress all the wrongs done to them, yet they must weigh the situation and deal with it skillfully. They must be careful not to claim Tibetan independence or disapprove of Party rule. Their attitude toward the newly established tourism association at Moluo Village also speaks of this political ingenuity. The township government founded this association in an effort to make peace with the villagers by allowing them to manage tourism on their own. However, local elites and some villagers assert that this is a devious strategy intended to transfer the township government's duties as administrator of tourism to the Moluo villagers and thus avoid the inevitable frictions over tourism interests. One villager even uses a Chinese idiom to describe this phenomenon: "playing off the barbarians against each other" (yiyizhiyi). Nevertheless, some key members of the tourism association, as well as many ordinary villagers, realize that the association has provided a legal framework within which they can push their claims for the queendom and other tourism agendas further. It also gives them a means of minimizing the township's interference as much as possible while recognizing its leadership in name only, allowing them to enjoy any benefits, will be distributed through township cadres.

The queendom dispute invokes and enhances the common identity of the people of Suopo, who feel ill-treated by the county and who must fight together for their rights. Their collective identity is based on geopolitical affiliation and differentiation: Suopo Township as a unit of solidarity versus its rival neighbor Zhonglu and other townships and also versus county authorities. However, on the issues of who are the more authentic Suopowa and who have more justifiable and legitimate claims to descent from ancient noble queens, Suopo is divided. The most noticeable boundary marker is the Dadu River, which bisects Suopo. Another marker is the Zangzu-Han difference. Zangzu villagers from the two sections on the eastern side of the Dadu River consider themselves to be the more authentic Suopowa and bearers of the queens' heritage compared to those on the western side, who formed close historical ties with those on the eastern bank only after 1950 and were merged into Suopo Township in 1992. The Han immigrants, referred to as "the Han Gang" by their Zangzu neighbors, make up a little more than 6 percent of the Suopo population; they constitute a marginal layer of the Suopowa identity but are completely excluded from the queendom identity. Finally, an underlying male-versus-female struggle plays out in complex ways in the queendom dispute.

## HEY, THE QUEENDOM IS OURS!

Not all villagers in Suopo know what the Eastern Queendom is, and some have never even heard of it. The legend of the queens is very popular, however, and they know that Suopo, along with a much larger region, used to be ruled by elegant queens who had the palace built at Jiadu (Suopo), in the midst of thick, dark forests, flanked by formidable cliffs on three sides. And they all believe that Zhonglu Township is "stealing" their queendom. Most do not blame the Zhonglu villagers and instead believe that county officials are responsible. The direct target is Mr. Tashi, a Zhonglu native and head of the cultural station, which is administered by the Culture and Tourism Bureau of Danba County. He is said to have taken advantage of his position to elevate Zhonglu as the site of the queen's palace, with another Zhongluwa standing behind him—Mr. Tsering, then vice-head of the county government and incumbent head of the county's People's Congress. The two Zhonglu natives, especially Mr. Tsering, are said to have manipulated their wide connections with other key county officials, who then voted for Zhonglu. Several representatives have been to the county seat on behalf of Suopo and accused the officials of favoritism.

The villagers' sense of frustration and unfairness has been channeled and guided by elites, who include local cadres, teachers, government employees, village heads, Bon priests and lamas, and others who have ample social and/ or financial resources at their disposal and thus the power to have their voices heard in the village. In the relatively egalitarian local environment, however, there is no clear-cut line distinguishing elites, whose authority is sometimes challenged.[6] On the whole, local elites tend to be more keen on the queendom issue than other villagers.

Of the queendom advocates, Uncle Pema, a cadre of Suopo Township, is the best known in and outside of Suopo. Nicknamed the "King of the Eastern Queendom," he has devoted most of his time and energy to publicizing Suopo as the "authentic" site of the ancient queens' palace. One of his colleagues comments, "Uncle Pema cares about nothing but 'his queendom'." Very often, when I entered his room at the township, he was talking to villagers about "his queendom." I became one of his most loyal listeners, listening to him talk for hours about his favorite topic. Each narrative is literally the same: queendom legends; the analysis of why Suopo, not Zhonglu, is the site of the queens' palace; his squabbles with Mr. Tashi and encounters with Mr. Wang, one of the most important leaders in Ganzi Tibetan Autonomous Prefecture; and his interactions with scholars and the media, for whom he acts as local guide and queendom counsel. Uncle Pema's queendom research may contribute to Suopo's tourism development, so township leaders have freed him from most administrative work, giving him time to pursue his own interests. He is also assigned to assist the township government's head of tourism development in Suopo, especially in Moluo Village, the only village in Ganzi prefecture and Danba County that has been rated a Famous Historical and Cultural Village in China. In this way, Uncle Pema is recognized not only by the township as the queendom expert whose knowledge it can use for tourism's sake but also by most villagers as the spokesman for their queendom due to his position as a township cadre and his courage in accusing the county authorities of favoritism.

In 2005, Uncle Pema's newspaper article on the discovery of the queendom palace in Suopo rocked the county and even the prefecture, calling the county's stance on the Zhonglu queendom into question. Since then, he has been a determined defender of the Suopo queendom cause. He is confident that he will be able to collect enough evidence to authenticate his claim but worries that Zhonglu officials may find ways to prevent the truth from being revealed. Uncle Pema asserts that major county officials, including the Party secretary, have recognized the legitimacy of Suopo's claim but that propaganda and publicity lag behind, while Zhonglu continues to appropriate the queendom label that rightfully belongs to Suopo. According to him, the reason for Mr. Tashi's unethical behavior is that he has made a large investment in his hostel in Zhonglu and thus will not easily give up the lucrative queendom trademark.

Uncle Pema takes every opportunity to propagandize his version of the queendom legends and to relay the evidence he has gathered, especially to scholars, whom he considers to be unbiased. He is always eager to share his queendom expertise with visiting university teachers and scholars, in the hope that his petitions will be publicized through these scholars' writings. He also avails himself of the media to trumpet his queendom cause as newspapers, magazines, and TV stations move in because of Danba's increasing prominence in the Chinese tourism market. However, he became frustrated with some of the "irresponsible" media who sought to determine the agenda themselves instead of unveiling what he saw as historical truth.[7] At one time, he was very interested in promoting the queendom to tourists and would meet them at the Suopo Bridge, volunteering to guide them and recount queendom legends. A local guide told me that on one occasion, his guests got so tired of Uncle Pema's harangue that they rudely told him to stop. This "indifference" has dampened his enthusiasm for publicizing the queendom to "unserious" and "uneducated" tourists.

Uncle Pema is fully aware that generating support among local villagers is essential for the success of his queendom cause. After all, his career is rooted in Suopo, and without the villagers' collaboration, he would not be able to regain his proprietorship of the queendom. As a Suopo native, he has wide connections among villagers. He is a hospitable host, and his room is often filled with villager guests who have come to the township on business. After offering them tea, he always takes the opportunity to lead his visitors into the world of the mythic queendom. Likewise, when he meets villagers on other occasions, it is not unusual for him to broach this subject. Unaffected by the sarcastic connotation of his "honorary" title, King of the Eastern Queendom, he persists in his campaign. His promotion of the queendom cause and determination to fight against county authorities have made him a rising star in Suopo Township. In his late fifties, he is now too old to run for township head after failing to be elected vice-head several years ago. "If I were younger, I could be [elected as] the head of the township government," Uncle Pema sighed. Indeed, his popularity has increased so dramatically that he might be able to secure enough support from the villagers.

In Uncle Pema's accounts of his queendom cause, he emphasizes Mr. Tashi's "piracy" and "spurious" claim that Zhonglu is the locus of the queens' palace. His sharp criticism and emotionally charged narration always evoke laughter and empathy from Suopo listeners. According to him, his solid evidence of the "authenticity" of his queendom-at-Suopo claim has often left Mr. Tashi speechless. Uncle Pema's proof is drawn mainly from popular legends, current place-names, existing relics, analysis of the geography and topography, and historical accounts. He claims that legends and place-names that build direct connections with the queendom cannot be found in Zhonglu; the greater number of stone watchtowers in Suopo shows that it is a more strategically important location, while Zhonglu is topographically unfit and arid; and various aspects of Suopo are more in accordance with Chinese historical accounts of the Eastern Queendom from ancient times, such as the architecture, wide use of hide boats, and the girls' puberty ritual.

Mr. Tashi, whom I have come to know well, argues that it is possible that the queens built their summer or winter palace in Zhonglu. Thus, Suopo and Zhonglu could band together to promote the queendom label. Uncle Pema firmly rejects this suggestion, arguing that Mr. Tashi has invested a lot of money in tourism and would benefit greatly from a tourism boom.

Uncle Pema convinced representatives of the county's People's Congress from Suopo, who are also village Party secretaries, to submit the proposal on the queendom (including the stone watchtowers) to the congress, but he is dissatisfied with the inaction of the congress and the county authorities at large. He suspects that Mr. Tashi and the Zhonglu clique in the county have set up a barrier to resolving this issue in favor of Suopo. Uncle Pema has considered posting a list of Mr. Tashi's misdeeds on every corner in the county seat so that Danba residents can judge for themselves. His position may seem radical to some, but his uncompromising style has made him a grassroots leader in Suopo.

Other village elites have played important roles in publicizing and popularizing the queendom discourse inside and outside of Suopo. Teacher Dorje and Teacher Namkha are two of these enthusiasts and proponents. Both are retired primary-school teachers with stable pensions.

Teacher Dorje has hosted the girls' puberty ritual several times since the late 1990s at so-called cultural festivals organized by the county. Due to his connections with county officials and knowledge of local customs and traditions, he is often asked to guide and host the VIPs and media representatives who visit Suopo, and he uses these occasions to promote the queendom and local culture. According to him, Gyarong culture is distinguished from those of other Zangzu subgroups by its "women's culture." However, the evidence that he uses to sustain his claim is almost exclusively from Suopo. He maintains that the essence of women's culture in Suopo is reflected in legends and customs that revolve around the queen and women as well as in the prestige of women in family and social matters. Like Uncle Pema, he has collected many legends about the queendom. He also suggests that many current customs in Suopo, such as the girls' puberty ritual, have been passed down from the queendom period.

The girls' puberty ritual used to be prepared for girls who reached the age of seventeen. During the New Year celebrations, villagers and relatives gathered together at the local monastery for this ceremony, and the girls wore their best clothes and fanciest jewelry. A poor family might borrow these things from relatives or neighbors. An important part of the ritual was that older women would help the girls style their hair in a unique way that few nowadays have mastered. It normally took half a day or more to arrange the hair in the shape of the two horns of the Khyung, the legendary bird in Tibetan tradition. According to Uncle Pema and Teacher Dorje, an ancient queendom tradition regarded the Khyung as its totem. This ritual was discontinued during the Cultural Revolution and was not revived until the late 1990s. These days, the primary purpose of the ritual is performance for tourists and media at the county's cultural festivals. Due to the lack of eligible girls, those who attend the ritual are not always seventeen-year-olds. In fact, some are married with children. Nevertheless, Teacher Dorje, among other local elites and some villagers, has declared to outsiders that this tradition was never diluted, that it is an essential part of local life, and that it represents a lineage connection with the ancient queens. This ritual has become the primary proof of the claim that local women are treated differently and more respectfully than in other cultures.

Teacher Dorje argues that in local tradition, women have enjoyed a prominent political position rarely seen in the Han and in other Zangzu regions. As every queendom advocate does, he cites the example of the three women who were received by Mao in recognition of their leadership skills, organizing capabilities, and working spirit. In Teacher Dorje's view, these Suopo women's achievements are inseparable from local cultural traditions that foster women's leadership capabilities and political wisdom and show that only Suopo is qualified to reclaim the queendom lineage.

Teacher Dorje claims that the county has not taken Suopo seriously or promoted it wholeheartedly. Sometimes, the county has even used the cultural resources and natural scenery of Suopo to advertise Zhonglu. In 2006, the Culture and Tourism Bureau asked him to guide a TV program team whose agenda was to shoot the site of the queendom in Suopo. The shoot lasted more than seven days. He had received the itinerary for the shoot but did not read it until the day he returned home. Only then did he realize that although the crew had shot footage in Suopo, the film would be presented as showing Zhonglu. He was so angry that he hurried to the county seat to confront the head of the Culture and Tourism Bureau and the film crew leader. Despite their claim that this was an accident, he assumed that county officials from Zhonglu had planned to do this all along. He was outraged but relieved that he had discovered the deception and protested. As he said, "If I hadn't seen this plan, I would have been thought of as a 'malefactor' [zuiren] to Suopo."

Teacher Namkha, another retired teacher, is a close friend of Uncle Pema's. Whenever they meet, their conversation on the queendom is endless. Teacher Namkha has collected hundreds of books in Chinese, which is very unusual even at the Danba County seat, not to mention in the countryside. Those he loves most are on Tibetan and Chinese history and culture. He attempts to reconstruct the history of the queendom through his understanding of these books and has written several articles on the queendom and local customs. His son, a dancer in the prefectural performing troupe, helps him type and edit his texts and post them on the Internet. A European specialist on stone watchtowers, who is engaged in the preservation of local cultural heritage, has asked Teacher Namkha to write on local tradition and also sent him a digital camera for shooting the scenery, folk customs, and anything else he thinks relevant. As he is a retired teacher with a good pension, purchasing a digital camera would not have been difficult for him; however, he cherishes this camera because it symbolizes international recognition of Suopo's unique cultural heritage. He has grown more infatuated with exploring and promoting local culture, reasoning that if a foreign scholar can travel so far to study Suopo, there is no excuse for him, a literate local, not to be fully engaged.

I befriended these three men and listened to their thoughts and ideas about the queendom, tourism development, cultural preservation, village politics, and so on. Common themes in their accounts are the uniqueness of Suopo traditions and the county government's indifference. For them, what makes Suopo stand out in Danba, in Zangzu regions, and in all of China is its "women's culture," as phrased by Teacher Dorje. All of them continually reminded me of the three women village leaders from Suopo who were received by Chairman Mao. They emphasized that only a most extraordinary person could be selected for such an honor, and it was remarkable that three people from the same township had received this opportunity. Even more unusual is that they were all women. These elite men point out that Suopo has the right soil for nurturing extremely beautiful, smart, and capable women who usually have the final say in family and village matters. They see this tradition as having come down from the ancient Eastern Queendom, not acknowledging the special circumstances of the 1950s and 1960s—the shortage of men in the village and the Party's promotion of the gender-equality ideology that made women's political prominence possible.

These three feel that the "glorious past" (represented by the above-mentioned women) has been ignored by the county government and have concluded that modern media could publicize their cause. In their encounters with correspondents and photographers from newspapers, magazines, and television stations, Uncle Pema and Teacher Dorje came to realize that some media just want something sensational, not the truth. Even worse, some use the footage shot in Suopo to advertise Zhonglu. They hope, however, to come across what they call "serious" media that can accurately present Suopo and its queendom. They also hope that scholars doing in-depth research can help publicize their cause. They all say that because they are not well educated, it is difficult for them to write and promote their ideas, so the impartial scholars will write about and for Suopo. After observing the popularity of the Internet at the Danba County seat in the past several years and its use by tourists, they have come to believe in its power. As

Teacher Namkha, whose son uploads his articles on the Internet, argued, there is much less "political check" on the Internet compared to other state-owned media. Another advantage is its wide distribution.

Many other elites are also actively involved in the queendom cause. As mentioned, two Suopo representatives in Danba County's People's Congress, who are also Party secretaries in their respective villages, submitted their queendom proposal to the congress and went to the county seat with Uncle Pema to question authorities about their favoritism. Several other Party secretaries and village heads, as well as some other elites, joined in this endeavor. The reactions of village VIPs toward the "biased" county government have influenced how villagers view this controversy. Uncle Pema's dramatic portrayal of his "battles" with Mr. Tashi and with the "dark" forces intent on marginalizing Suopo has won their sympathy. This is partially because elites tend to have social capital or resources—such as money, power, *guanxi* (communal kinship ties and networks of personal connections), and education—and/or are in respectable professions (lama, teacher, cadre) that privilege their words and actions.

Nonetheless, the villagers' judgments and decisions are not always guided by elites but based on their own evaluation of situations. Their participation in the queendom effort is inseparable from their resentment toward the county and township governments for delays in resolving the Suopo Bridge issue and other concerns. The assumed unfairness and favoritism in the queendom issue just reconfirms their marginalized status in Danba and their expectation of being neglected by county cadres. The villagers' expressions of hostility or frustration are thus understandable and widely shared.

Elites play a role in channeling these popular expressions, either moderating or intensifying them. In certain circumstances, when elites feel it necessary to counter a deteriorating situation, they may take advantage of their social capital and direct others toward appeasement through coercion or other means; under other circumstances, they may choose to provoke others to heighten the tension. In Suopo, elites see the intensification of the situation as an opportunity to reject the county government's agenda and retrieve what had belonged to Suopo exclusively. What can elites gain from this?

Uncle Pema declares that what he does has nothing to do with his personal interests, and he anticipates no rewards from tourism. He claims to be working to benefit the people of Suopo and to satisfy his pride in the local queendom heritage. However, other villagers drew my attention to the fact that his hostility toward Mr. Tashi is connected with disputes over the construction of Uncle Pema's eldest son's new house in Moluo Village several years ago. Their old house was some twenty meters away from a stone watchtower, and they were going to build the new one at the original site. However, Mr. Tashi stopped them because, according to the county's new regulations on watchtower protection and safety, new houses built in Moluo must be more than fifty meters away from watchtowers. Although Uncle Pema finally managed to have the new house built after persistently petitioning the head of the Culture and Tourism Bureau, and after several clashes with Mr. Tashi, he lost the opportunity to collaborate with a European specialist who was said to have agreed to sponsor the construction because she wanted a room in which to live. As a consequence of Uncle Pema's prolonged disputes with Mr. Tashi, she purchased a house in another village instead and is said to have invested ¥40,000 ($6,265) in building a new village road. That being so, Uncle Pema sees Mr. Tashi as the one who spoiled this golden chance.

Uncle Pema's other two children, a son and a daughter, expect that they will benefit eventually from tourism development in Moluo. This son is a member of the newly founded tourism association in Moluo, and his wife sometimes sells local produce to tourists or serves as a guide. Uncle Pema's daughter and her husband are building a huge house at the entrance to the village, hoping that it can be turned into a hostel when tourism increases.

Teacher Dorje has invested in tourism, too. He opened one of the earliest hostels in Moluo and also plans to turn the newly finished house for his eldest son into a hostel when the time is ripe. It is expected that with the publicity of the queendom label and subsequent inflow of tourists, locals will benefit directly and the village Party secretary and village head, who endorse this cause, may be rewarded with the villagers' trust and support. It is likely that some of them, if not all, will benefit from tourism directly. For instance, one of the village leaders recently had a "mansion" built—the largest and most luxurious house in Suopo, which can accommodate more than a hundred tourists.

Most Suopo elites are invested in the queendom cause in one way or another with the expectation of being rewarded for their dedication. To quote one villager, "Why wouldn't they [elites] care about the Eastern Queendom? How could it be possible for them to do something that they will not benefit from?" This is almost a standard belief among villagers as to the motives of these elites. Many villagers gave me examples of how village heads or other elites used their power, money, and social connections to serve their interests. Compared to elites, common villagers are at a disadvantage. To quote another villager: "They [Uncle Pema and the two retired teachers] have nothing else to do. They are cadres. Just sit there and get the money. Unlike them, we are peasants, no money, no *guanxi* . We have to toil very hard every day from morning till evening. How can we afford the time and energy for that [the queendom cause]?" As this villager claims, the unequal distribution of social resources between elites and villagers results in their different degrees of dedication. There are, however, villagers who are also very keen on the queendom cause.

Reward and possible benefits from the cause are more than economic and include prestige and status in the village. Uncle Pema takes pride in his rise to prominence as the "King of the Eastern Queendom." Teacher Dorje said he almost would have "committed a crime" if he hadn't discovered the TV program's deceptive plan of substituting Zhonglu for Suopo. "How would I have the 'face' [courage] to live in the village? All the people would curse me for bringing these people here!" he exclaimed.

Then Teacher Namkha said, "We cannot leave the heritage of our ancestors unattended. I am getting old. How many more years can I live? I don't know. I just want to make use of the time collecting folk stories and customs and taking photos. I will leave all these [writings] and all my books for later generations, whether they want them or not. Maybe one day when they see them by chance, they will be amazed at what a splendid culture our Suopo once had."

The villagers' concern for reputation and pride in their local heritage, often accompanied by anxiety over its possible disappearance, are significant, as are their concerns about the queendom and pride in their collective identity as Suopowa who share "unique" traditions along with their marginalized status in Danba. Some say openly that if the county government does not treat them justly by restoring the queendom label, they will take extreme actions by demonstrating and appealing collectively to the prefecture, province, and, finally, to Beijing if the issues are not resolved. As one villager alleged, "This is the sky of the Chinese Communist Party. Big blue sky! The county government cannot darken it. There is always somewhere we can appeal in order to get justice. I just don't believe a little county like Danba would rebel [against the Party]!"

An important message conveyed here is the view that the center, Beijing, is an embodiment of absolute justice, while the periphery, Danba, is corrupt. This dynamism in the relationship between the center and the periphery is not unusual in a highly centralized state; in the Soviet Union as well, the people at the periphery often looked to the center (i.e., Moscow or a deified national leader like Stalin) for final justice (see, e.g., Brandenberger 2005).

Two important factors contribute to this phenomenon: first, turning to an omnipotent and merciful godlike ruler "high above" enables the marginalized to voice their pains in a highly centralized society where the outlet for accumulated grievances is limited; second, thanks to successful ideological inculcation campaigns, marginal peoples are convinced (or made to believe) that the center is their final hope for a better future. In China, the themes "Only the Communist Party can save China" and "The Central Party Committee is the great savior that will rescue Han commoners and especially minorities from the hellish pre-Liberation feudalism or serfdom" reverberate in the media, textbooks, official documents, and political meetings. Through incessant propaganda, the central government has also impressed both the Han minorities with its efforts to crack down on local cadre corruption and delinquency, conveying the message that the problem is always local and the center is the savior. These factors are instrumental in enlisting support for the central state from Suopo villagers and others.

Nevertheless, it would be simplistic to assume that the central Party-state as the ultimate source of justice is merely imaginary. The past decade has seen notable improvements in traffic and communication, educational, and other basic facilities in Danba, and local farmers have benefited from substantial government subsidies and preferential policies oriented toward the development of Zangzu regions. Thus, Zangzu locals have "tasted the sweetness," and their support of the central Party-state is not an unexpected outcome. Although it is true that material gains won't always engender loyalty among minorities, including the Zangzu and Uyghur, it is fair to say that economic and rural reforms do bring about positive change in the countryside, as millions of farmers in China acknowledge. Although these reforms have also caused increasing rural unrest, most collective actions target local state agencies, corporations, factories, and individuals, not the central government.

Why has the local state become the target of the villagers' anger in Danba and other places in China? Local officials and cadres are the ones who implement policies made by the central state and other higher authorities, and they must then interact directly with the grass roots. In the process of carrying out these policies, conflicts with villagers are inevitable. The opinion of both Danba cadres and villagers that the policies of the central government are very good explains some of the contention in Danba. County and township cadres often complained to me that "too many" preferential policies for local villagers have made the latter accustomed to "free subsidies." Without the constant inflow of financial or material support, the villagers would blame the county or township for being irresponsible and not doing its job or even for corruption. Simultaneously, it was impossible to distribute these benefits equally among villagers due to the limited amounts available and governmental agendas of providing special aid to certain groups such as the elderly, the disabled, or the poor. As a result, many villagers protested the "uneven" or "unfair" distribution. Since the county and especially the township oversaw the distribution of most subsidies, they naturally became the targets of local ire. From the point of view of many villagers, the present cadres are different from or the opposite of the pre-1980s cadres, who were said to be conscientious, altruistic, responsible, hardworking, and sympathetic.

The fact that conflicts have intensified in the past decade, especially in the past five years, as exemplified by the frequency and scale of collective action in Danba, is consistent with an overall increase in discord in rural China.[8] Most scholars agree that this has much to do with general political relaxation and the segmentation of officialdom or the state.[9] As is the case everywhere in China, Danba locals are finding more avenues for self-expression. The opening of such avenues is partly the result of the shift in the state-society relationship as societal sectors expand in scale and influence in spite of the unshaken Party- and state-centric ruling approach in China (Perry 2010); it also derives from the fact that some state officials and cadres "are disposed to champion popular demands" rather than invariably siding with the state (O'Brien 2002, 151).

Uncle Pema himself is a state employee who has been able to get along with almost all the other township cadres, especially the Party secretary and township head. He has kept the Party secretary—the most important leader in the township—informed of his plans for the queendom, his conflicts with

Mr. Tashi, and his petitions to county authorities. According to Uncle Pema, his actions were approved by the Party secretary, who, however, warned him to be cautious. In my conversations with the township cadres, they all seemed in favor of Uncle Pema's queendom project, though their support was most often merely verbal. I later learned that some didn't really care much about this project, since it had little do with their work or political careers; however, they considered it "politically correct" to express their verbal support. This reserved support is based on their assessment of the situation: directly opposing the queendom project would invite criticism from Suopo villagers and offend their friendly colleague Uncle Pema, yet supporting the project publicly would likely invite negative ratings from county authorities who are often the target of the villagers' extreme actions.

Another important factor is that although township leaders did show interest in the queendom project and hoped to involve themselves even more, the lack of institutional and economic resources forestalled any action other than verbal support. Development of tourism and cultural heritage is always administered and monitored by the county's Culture and Tourism Bureau, and oftentimes the township government is expected only to assist the bureau in its work. The township often feels a sense of power-lessness as a result of its subordinate or supporting role in relation to county agencies. This affected its involvement in the queendom project. Suopo Township also had very limited administrative fees appropriated by the county government each year, which were used specifically for administra-tive matters and receptions for visiting county cadres and others. Thus, it had no extra money for developing this or other projects. It must apply to various county agencies for funding. The *guanxi* between township heads and county officials is sometimes an important factor in townships being funded. That is why even if Suopo Township leaders did want to support their villagers in the queendom dispute, they hesitated to fully endorse the Suopowa's claim for fear of creating a strained relationship with county authorities.

As a result, championing this popular demand verbally and prudently is the middle way and thus the best way for the township to follow. The reac-tions of the township's cadres to the queendom project also reveal that local state actors have their own agendas and interests; their decisions and choices are constrained by the concrete situation and are based on their thorough evaluation of the situation.

## "EMBARRASSED" HAN ON THE MARGIN

The queendom cause is a collective battle of Suopo villagers against the "prej-udiced" county government. In this process, the Suopowa identity is fortified and invoked as a close-knit community that shares language, culture, terri-tory, queendom lineage, and the common experience and destiny of being residents of an executive subdivision of Danba. In this way, the Suopowa are defined genealogically (blood and ancestry), culturally (language and cul-ture), and administratively (under the jurisdiction of Suopo Township). Then who are the "authentic" Suopowa? How is the boundary of this category marked? The answer involves different degrees or scopes of internal identi-fication. Originally, the term "Suopowa" referred only to the natives of the Suopo segment (the villages of Nongzhong and Gongbu), next to the Dazhai segment (the villages of Moluo, Zuobi, Basuo, and Laiyi) on the eastern side of the Dadu River. In 1950, a township named after the Suopo segment was founded in newly established Danba County to administer these two seg-ments. The scope of the concept "Suopowa" was thus extended to Dazhai, which constitutes the second layer of the Suopowa identity. After the Pujia-oding segment with four villages on the western side of the Dadu River merged with Suopo Township in 1992, this concept expanded to include these four villages, making up the third layer of the Suopowa identity. Suopo Township's eleventh village, Dongfeng, is normally referred to as a Suopo segment, but its people, most of whom are Han immigrants, are not classified as Suopowa in most circumstances since they have no roots in Suopo. None-theless, in some situations, they are recognized by other villagers as Suo-powa, though in a very loose sense, which accounts for the fourth layer (see fig. 4.1). After all, as residents of the same township, Dongfeng villagers share some common experiences with local Zangzu villagers, such as enmity toward the township and county governments. Consequently, a question arises: Does the queendom-at-Suopo campaign concern them?

Regarding the Dongfeng villagers' status in Suopo Township, a county cadre once commented, "Others [Zangzu Suopo villagers] think of them as beggars." "It is we who are really the minority here," said a Dongfeng vil-lager. According to one of my eldest informants, who was in her eighties, at the time of Liberation in Danba in 1950, there were only three Han house-holds comprising about ten people. Driven by endless warfare and starva-

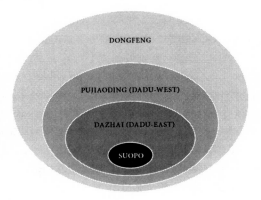

FIG. 4.1. The Suopowa identity

tion, they had fled here from other parts of Sichuan. After Liberation, more Han moved in, and now the Han population in Dongfeng is 215, accounting for roughly 6.5 percent of Suopo's total population. Except for a few Zangzu villagers who married in, all are Han or mixed-blood persons who are usually identified as "Zangzu" on their residence registration cards. In the other ten villages in Suopo Township, however, almost all residents are Zangzu. As a way of distinguishing themselves from the Donfengwa, the residents of the other ten villages normally refer to the Dongfeng villagers as the Han Gang, a term with negative connotations, designating these "rootless" people who are "different from us" in terms of their culture and mind-set and who do not belong to or own this land.[10] In the 1960s, Dongfeng—with the most barren land in Suopo—merged with Moluo and became one "production brigade" (*shengchan dadui*). Having grown more and more disgruntled with the fact that the Donfengwa would be sharing their fertile land and diluting their work points,[11] the Moluowa persistently petitioned the township and county government for a split; three years later, they were able to banish all of the Han Gang except for two households.[12] As Dongfeng's population began to grow, the villagers started to expand their land downward to Moluo and upward to Gongbu. People from these two villages complained about this "shameless invasion."

I often heard from Zangzu villagers that the Dongfengwa are clever in comparison to local Zangzu, meaning that the Donfengwa and Han at large are believed to have "economic minds" (*jingji tounao*): they, unlike the Zangzu, have learned how to make money. However, such words are not always used as praise. On the contrary, they imply pragmatism, selfishness, slyness, calculation, money hunger, and untrustworthiness. Some Zangzu villagers also believe that the Donfengwa do not possess virtues, such as caring for others or filial piety (*xiao*), since they assume that the Dongfengwa have no religion and thus do not worry about bad karma. However, many Zangzu villagers do recognize the Dongfengwa's strength. I often hear from Zangzu villagers that the Donfengwa are more hardworking than they are, and they express their admiration for the importance the Han attach to education. Nevertheless, the Dongfengwa do not recognize these qualities as virtuous because they have no choice but to be strong. As one Dongfeng villager in his early sixties said,

> The policy toward Zangzu is very good. We [Dongfengwa] don't have [the same policy] . . . we all do odd jobs at other places. Our land is very infertile. For Zangzu, they just expect "the pie to fall from the sky" [*tianshang diao xianbing*]. What do they worry about? The state will take care of them. . . . I sent all three of my children to school, and they have all become cadres in other counties [of Ganzi Tibetan Autonomous Prefecture]. What can we do? If they didn't go to school, how would they feed themselves here? . . . I will labor here for a few more years. Then I will leave for good.

His impression of Zangzu villagers is shared by many other Dongfengwa, who feel that their Zangzu neighbors can simply wait for governmental support and do nothing. That is why they can be lazy. Some Dongfengwa also believe that many Zangzu locals are very dirty and stupid. "I am asked to plaster their new houses," said a Dongfeng villager. "Zangzu just cannot do it. They are unable to make the surface [of the wall] smooth. They never learn."

With both sides inclined to distrust and even to despise each other, how can Zangzu villagers expect the Dongfengwa to contribute to the queendom cause? Indeed, most Dongfengwa simply don't care about it. They reside on this piece of land, but many don't feel fully connected to it, so the legend about the queen that can be traced back more than a thousand years has nothing to do with them. Zangzu villagers don't bother to engage the Donfengwa in the queendom cause because the Dongfengwa are not qualified to claim any connection with the noble and elegant queens of the past.

Connection with the queendom is not, however, the only criterion for being identified as "Suopowa." Despite the fact that most Zangzu villagers do not count their Han neighbors as "authentic" Suopowa, they do share common interests and experiences as residents of the same township and often need to work together. Thus, the Dongfengwa are also part of the Suopowa although they are at the most peripheral layer of this identification. The Suopo Bridge issue is a common concern for the seven villages on the eastern side of the Dadu River, including Dongfeng. Like other villagers, the Dongfengwa condemn the inefficiency and favoritism of county officials.

The Dongfengwa raised another common issue, the gold mine that has affected four neighboring villages (Dongfeng, Gongbu, Nongzhong, and Moluo), and inspired their Zangzu neighbors to follow suit. The situation became so intense and confrontational that it convulsed the whole county. One night in May 2007, a detonation at the gold mine nearby caused cracks in some houses in Dongfeng. Led by the village head, most of villagers, some 140, stormed over to the gold mine to argue with its owner. Township cadres tried unsuccessfully to resolve the conflict. Dongfeng villagers accused the township's Party secretary and governmental heads of taking bribes from the gold mine's owner. Tension with the township escalated to the extent that two villagers drove the Party secretary into the Dadu River.[13] Not until the owner promised to compensate villagers for the damage did they back down.

One former village head admired the Dongfengwa's courage so much that he claimed that "we Zangzu are just like a pile of loose sand. Look at them [the Dongfengwa]. How united they are! We should learn from them." Then Zangzu villagers did learn. With Dongfeng as their model, villagers in Gongbu and Nongzhong organized two big protests involving more than a hundred participants. They pressured the gold mine owner for more compensation by smashing machines and installations, and they demonstrated at the county government intermittently for a month. That is why some cadres argue that the Suopowa are the "wildest" of Zangzu, yet this expression of opinion by Zangzu villagers in Suopo owes much to the Dongfengwa's pioneering public display of outrage. With their actions, the Dongfengwa proved that they deserved to live there after all.

In a narrow sense, the Dongfengwa are not dedicated to the queendom, but the queendom dispute is entangled with other issues. The primary issues concern how the Suopowa themselves think of and respond to social changes and political reforms as a way in which to highlight their own identity as an internally bounded collective worthy of attention and respect, even at the cost of clashing with higher authorities. By virtue of this public demonstration of collective identity, Dongfeng villagers also contributed to the queendom cause by challenging the partisanship and nepotism of county authorities. Although a causal relationship between the Dongfeng-wa's protest and the ensuing protests of their Zangzu neighbors cannot be proved, it is fair to say that the Dongfengwa's act of defying authority spurred Zangzu villagers to act. Many Zangzu villagers applaud the Dong-fengwa's daring and intrepidness. Most villagers believe that the county and township governments "bully the weak and fear the strong" (*qiruan paying*) and that if they continue to be as passive and obedient as in the past, they will never win respect from the county. Neither will they win back their queendom label. So some openly express the possibility of taking extreme actions if the county government continues to turn a deaf ear to their pleas. In this way, the Dongfengwa have been instrumental in inflaming the queendom dispute, which is not their direct concern.

Nonetheless, the "embarrassed" status of the Dongfengwa in Suopo has been reinforced rather than ameliorated through the queendom cause. Although the Dongfengwa's rebellious spirits serve as a model for their neighbors in the intensifying struggle with the county, the queendom identity leaves no place for the Dongfengwa. Roughly parallel to the different layers of "Suopowa" identification, the queendom identity has layers, too, which are defined by degrees of connection and proximity to the legendary queendom. Of the three segments of the township, the Suopo segment and the Dazhai segment are equally linked with the queendom. Although the claimed palace of the queens is located in the Suopo segment, these two segments have always been connected internally through kinship and marital exchange. Thus, both share a direct lineage with the queens. This is the first layer of queendom identity. The four villages on the western side of the Dadu River seldom shared ritual or public space where religious activities or other public events such as weddings and funerals took place, nor did marital exchange occur. This is largely a result of the obstruction of the Dadu River. After Liberation in 1950, these villages were first affiliated with another township before merging with Suopo Township. However, they share language and cultural traditions with the Suopo and Dazhai segments and thus are also assumed to be vaguely related to the queendom. This constitutes yet another layer of queendom identity. In contrast, the Zhon-

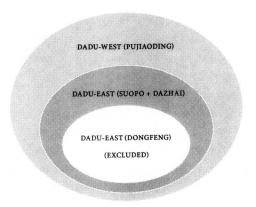

FIG. 4.2. The queendom identity

gluwa, who share the same language and traditions and also have had frequent interactions with the Suopo and Dazhai segments, are excluded from this identification. The queendom identity appears to be a primary reflection of Suopo localism, which stresses the exclusive connection of Suopo with the queendom. Since the Dongfengwa have different blood and traditions, they are completely cut off from this identification (see fig. 4.2).

Queendom identity is thus a local, or township, identity that the Suopowa assert so that they can distinguish themselves from other townships, especially their rival, Zhonglu. It is also a compartmentalized internal identity in that it distinguishes between its first and second layers based on their supposed degree of lineage and cultural purity in relation to the ancestral queens. Finally, it marks an unequivocal line between local Zangzu and the Han. Thus, the Zangzu-Han difference is crystallized in the queendom reconstruction process. As a consequence, the landscape of the queendom cause becomes more nuanced and convoluted (see fig. 4.3). On the one hand, this cause calls for coordination among all villagers (including the Dongfengwa) in order to concentrate their strength in fighting against Zhonglu "thieves" and county authorities. On the other hand, this cause that underscores lineage and cultural purity and authenticity anticipates different degrees of dedication from the two Zangzu wings, which are divided by the Dadu River. The Dongfengwa are further marked off from Suopo's cultural map and the queendom plan.

However, the Dongfengwa may also benefit from the queendom cause. With the development of tourism as a result of the queendom publicity, the

| Segments | Suopo Township | | | | Zhonglu Township |
|---|---|---|---|---|---|
| | Dadu-East | | | Dadu-West | |
| | Suopo | Dazhai | Dongfeng | Pujiaoding | |
| Suopowa Identity | ♦♦♦♦ | ♦♦♦ | ♦ | ♦♦ | × |
| Queendom Identity | ＊＊ | ＊＊ | × | ＊ | × |

Higher number of ♦ = Stronger Suopowa identity
Higher number of ＊ = Stronger queendom identity
× = Lack of Identity Link

FIG. 4.3. The combined Suopowa and queendom identity

Dongfengwa may turn to the tourism industry as well. This may lead to some conflict: if tourists come and pay for the "unique" queendom culture of Suopo, what is the position of the Dongfengwa who are not affiliated? Since the Dongfengwa can be very assertive and rebellious, how will they handle this situation? Will they acquiesce to taking on the status of a rootless group in Suopo? Considering the fact that they have had increasing conflicts with other villagers over water, land, and other issues, it is likely that they will not easily give up their pursuits. That is why some cadres and Zangzu villagers maintain that "the Dongfengwa are too wild." Since the Dongfengwa's unusual wildness derives from their agitation over their peripheral status in Suopo, any action that further marginalizes them may provoke even wilder expressions of anxiety caused by their rootlessness. The interaction between the "wildest" Zangzu villagers and the "too wild" Dongfengwa problematizes the prospects of the queendom discourse and complicates the sociopolitical landscape of Suopo.

In summary, the Suopowa's struggle for the queendom label is embedded in the social and political transformation of Danba and China in general, which is characterized by increasing collective actions of rural sectors against the local state apparatus and other sectors. In this process, Suopo villagers are engaged in an identity politics that aims to define their manifold identities along the lines of Chinese citizenship, interethnic and intraethnic sameness and differences, regional and local ties, professional and peasant status, marginality and majority perceptions, and other political stances such as loyalty to the Party-state. Elites have played an important role in channeling the villagers' perceptions of the queendom dispute and engaging them in the fight for "justice." The township's middle-way approach—verbally endorsing the queendom claim—is based largely on the cadres' evaluation of their relations with both locals and the county, which exhibits intrastate variations and the different interests and agendas of multiple state actors. The relationship between the Han Dongfengwa and Zangzu villagers, which is prominent in this struggle, reveals more than Han-Zangzu ethnic, cultural, and genealogical differences, and their mutual relationships are informed by political goals and interests. The Zangzu villagers, like local state officials, are far from being a homogenized whole. They are internally united and/or divided by locality, queendom lineage, and other political interests.

Chapter 5

# THE MOLUO TOURISM ASSOCIATION

## *How Far to Go?*

*

The Moluo Tourism Association is registered with the Civil Affairs Bureau and the Culture and Tourism Bureau of Danba County as a state-certified "popular association" (*minjian shetuan*). Although defined thus, it is not a purely voluntary or self-generating organization, since its founding was based on the "organizational will" (*zuzhi yitu*) of the local state in Danba, which expresses the intentions of the county bureaucracy. Its members are appointed or approved by the Party secretary of Suopo Township with the advice of his subordinate, Uncle Pema, the famous "King of the Eastern Queendom," and its activities are to be performed under the jurisdiction of the village committee. Despite the state's strong presence in the Moluo Tourism Association as well as the association's semiofficial nature, it is also a popular association because of the voluntary participation of eight villagers and the villagers' recognition of its role in coordinating efforts to develop tourism in Moluo. More than that, its members and some villagers use the tourism association as a legal mechanism for engaging in the queendom struggle and pressing other political claims. However, tourism association members have disparate positions on the association's relationship with local government and divergent development agendas. These differences are a continuation of everyday village tensions and negotiations.

Scholars point out that the concept of "civil society," which originated in European traditions and practices, doesn't translate easily into the sociopolitical, historical, and cultural contexts of China.[1] In China, hierarchy and *guanxi*, or communal kinship ties and networks of personal connections, often characterize various organizations and social groups. Simultaneously, due to the omnipresent influence of the state, most officially certified civil associations or nongovernmental organizations have adopted a conciliatory or cooperative attitude toward the powerful state and are not concerned primarily with seeking autonomy (see, e.g., Sujian Guo 2000; Weller 2005). Therefore, these organizations seem incompatible with the standard understanding of a civil society, which is thought to "(1) be voluntary, . . . based on the free choice of autonomous individuals; (2) act with civility, . . . accept the rights of others to disagree. . . . and (3) respect the legitimacy of the state while in turn enjoying a free space for action guaranteed by the state" (Weller 1999, 15). Thus, with the penetration of state power into social sectors, these social organizations and associations are not always "civil" in the Western sense. Nevertheless, they not only play a role similar to that of a civil society in connecting the family, community, and private spheres with the state but also can facilitate political change and generate space for civil dissent.[2]

The notion of the "state-led civil society" (Frolic 1997) has been suggested as a way of categorizing the "alternative" civil society in China, in which the Party-state exerts firm control over its societal sectors and the state takes advantage of its created civil society to "help it govern, co-opt and socialize potentially politically active elements in the population" (Saich 2004, 228). However, as evidenced by the Moluo Tourism Association, despite the imprint of state will, various associations in China may be able to secure a degree of free space and develop their own agendas, which consequently may pose a challenge to state agendas. In this way, the state and society display more nuanced interactions than mere opposition.

## POSITIONS OF TOURISM ASSOCIATION MEMBERS

The Moluo Tourism Association is the second and, at present, only officially recognized tourism association in Danba County. The Jiaju Tourism Association in Niega Township was disbanded—though not officially—after the 2006 Gelindeya incident, in which increasing tourism led to social and bureaucratic chaos. The founding of the Moluo Tourism Association in 2008 was built upon the lesson the county authorities learned from the failed experiment of engaging elites and villagers in tourism development projects. They feared that if the Party and the government allowed such a quasi–civil association to grow and define its own agenda freely, the situation would spin out of their control. With this legacy in mind, Mr. Chen, the Party secretary of Suopo Township, was cautious about the membership and guidelines for the Moluo Tourism Association. In reality, however, the association seems to be more than the county's or township's puppet. The eight members include Teacher Thubten, a well-respected retired teacher, who serves as the head; two vice-heads, Yeshe, a retired county cadre and successful businessman, and Tsering, a former accountant for the village committee who is known for his sophistication; Teacher Dorje, a retired schoolteacher and local cultural specialist; Lobsang, a retired cadre; and two young men and one middle-aged woman who are known for their singing and dancing talents.[3] Although these members are officially designated, they use the association as a legal framework that enables them to fight for their queendom cause, express their concerns about Moluo's tourism prospects, and explore the possibilities of promoting Moluo and Suopo to the outside world by going beyond the restrictions of local authorities.

These members take three different positions—which may be described as cooperative, radical, and passive—on the association's relationship with the township, publicizing their queendom discourse, and advertising Moluo's and Suopo's tourism resources.

The cooperative position stresses the essential importance of keeping the township government and village committee (the administrative body at the village) informed about the association's plans and activities while engaging villagers in the development of tourism in Moluo. Teacher Thubten stressed that the association must follow the guidelines set by the township and the village committee and also highlighted the importance of villager participation as well as the association's central tenet, which is to serve the villagers' interests.

The radical position is based on the incapability of and/or indifference of local authorities when it comes to promoting Suopo and thus advocates self-promotion in order to enlist support from and cooperate with the media, scholars, and other interested groups and individuals. Yeshe and several other members advocated such a stance with varying degrees of intensity. They blamed local authorities for doing little to help Suopo and Moluo and even obstructing their advancement; instead of cooperating with the authorities, they sought help from external sources. The radicals asserted that if Moluo did become famous due to their persistent promotion, the county and township governments should not involve themselves or share the benefits.

Finally, the passive position is characterized by a "nothing can be done about it" or "let it be" attitude, which is often accompanied by a sense of helplessness and a pessimistic view of the association's limited role. Teacher Dorje became so frustrated with shortsighted villagers whose desire for quick money took precedence over their concern for the queendom cultural heritage that he began to think that challenging their mentality was a nearly impossible task.

Nevertheless, some members shift their positions as the situation changes or react differently in various contexts. For instance, Teacher Dorje sometimes held a cooperative position and at other times became radical, claiming that the county and township governments should "leave Moluo alone" and that Moluowa would do whatever was best for themselves. From time to time, Teacher Thubten expressed his desire to quit the post and have nothing further to do with the association because of its powerless and awkward state. Despite their differences, all of the members agreed that external support was essential for publicizing their queendom cause and establishing their village and township as a worthy tourist attraction.

This association is also divided into two notable camps built on different interests and agendas. Yeshe, one of the retired cadres, makes up one camp all by himself; he has won the support from one other association member, a small number of villagers, and his relatives, including his nephew—a former village head who plans to run for the position again. The other camp consists of all the other members and is concerned about whether Yeshe will take over the association and turn it into a profit-making instrument for himself. Nonetheless, it is not a homogeneous collective. Everyone in this camp has his or her own ideas and plans for how the association should work. The opposition between the two camps is not derived wholly from the members' differences of opinion; it is rooted in daily village lives and histories. Therefore, the tourism association is just another field for the continuation or escalation of village conflicts.

Who is Yeshe and why has he taken such a position? How can he be a camp largely by himself? Yeshe is also not on good terms with the township cadres, who are accused of being irresponsible and incapable, while some cadres believe that he is too sly and complicated to deal with. If this is so, why did the township Party secretary make him the vice-head of the tourism association in the first place?

The majority of Moluo villagers have a negative view of Yeshe. The most frequent comment is that he is too selfish, yet all agree that he is smart enough to know how to make money. He used to work at the county's "science commission" (*kewei*). After retirement, he turned the barren land beside his house into an apple orchard. He sells the young trees to other peasants or to other counties in Ganzi Tibetan Autonomous Prefecture and also sells apples to fruit merchants. His other dealings include the sale of cattle, and some villagers claim that he might earn ¥100,000–200,000 (about $15,625–31,250) every year—a sum equal to the yearly income of at least ten average households. In many villagers' eyes, Yeshe cares only about money and not about the well-being of other villagers, nor does he seem interested in helping to lift his fellow villagers out of poverty. His selfish image was reinforced when he evaded responsibility for damage to twelve houses located below his fruit orchard caused by his nonstop irrigation since 2003. Four households had to build new houses at other locations, and two rebuilt them on the original site because of the lack of alternatives. Yeshe argued that the damage had nothing to do with him and that, on the contrary, without his fruit orchards, the situation could have been even worse because his hundreds of fruit trees solidify the soil and protect the environment. This claim has estranged him from other villagers, but his unshakable status as the wealthiest man in the village and township, his wide connections with county cadres, and his forceful eloquence, literacy, and knowledge of Party policies and the outside world make him a strong and even intimidating presence in Moluo and Suopo. Few can take him for granted. That is also the reason he was "elected" vice-head of the tourism association.

## MAKING THE MOLUO TOURISM ASSOCIATION

Most tourism association members say that they were elected by villagers. As a matter of fact, their nominations were approved by the township Party secretary, Mr. Chen, at the suggestion of Uncle Pema and Teacher Dorje after negotiations with fourteen seniors (over fifty years old), the village head, and the Party secretary.[4] By "elected," they meant that their membership was legitimate and supported by the masses and that they have the authority to speak for the villagers, whose interests they represent.

As mentioned, the county and township governments wanted to make sure that the tourism association, like other village associations, would be securely under their control because of the Gelindeya incident in Jiaju in 2006. The incident was caused by many problems that grew out of the increasing popularity of Jiaju, called "the most beautiful village in China," in the Chinese tourist market and the skyrocketing number of tourists who have traveled there since the early 2000s. Conflicts included local guides and tourist reception households (family hostels) fighting over tourists, overcharging for accommodations and guide fees, improperly discharging excrement and polluting drinking water, children begging tourists for money, a growing income gap between tourist reception households and non-tourist-reception households, and intensified disagreement between villagers, the township, and the county government over ticket income distribution. In 2006, CCTV (China Central Television Station), the most influential TV station in China, produced two episodes on the chaotic situation in Jiaju titled "Gelindeya."[5] As a result, the county heads were censured by prefectural officials for the disorder in Jiaju and their inability to keep the situation in check. The Ganzi prefecture government took the matter so seriously that it ordered all counties to conduct sessions of self-critique or self-examination so that they could learn from Danba's failure at managing tourism and governing its people, and the Danba County government had to launch an intensive self-criticism campaign. The county government put the blame on the Jiaju Tourism Association, whose three major leaders, trustworthy retired cadres from county agencies, had been appointed by the county's former Party secretary but were now accused of inciting villagers to defy the county government's authority. After this incident, the county and township governments marginalized the Jiaju Tourism Association by ceasing to involve it in Jiaju's tourism projects, although they have not yet officially disbanded the organization.

Construction of the tourism association in Moluo Village is part of the New Socialist Countryside Construction (Shehuizhuyi Xinnongcun Jianshe) project, a nationwide initiative launched by the central government that aims to transform China's rural areas mentally and materially.[6] Moluo's designation as one of the first two experimental sites for this project in

Danba in 2008 was inseparable from its status as Danba's only Famous Historical and Cultural Village of China. A claimed agenda of this rural development project is to promote democratic political construction at the grass roots—that is, within the legal framework of the Chinese state and under the leadership of the Chinese Communist Party, peasants are granted the rights of democratic elections (*minzhu xuanju*), democratic decision making (*minzhu juece*), democratic administration (*minzhu guanli*), and democratic superintendence (*minzhu jiandu*) as a way of involving them in the construction of the new countryside. The founding of the tourism association in Moluo was intended to make Moluo villagers take charge of their own tourism development. The Gelindeya incident cast a shadow over the newly founded tourism association, and the last thing the county and township governments wanted was for the association to turn against them by developing its own agendas and inciting villagers to protest.

Uncle Pema was entrusted by Mr. Chen, his superior and the township's Party secretary, with the task of nominating candidates for the tourism association, since it was assumed that Uncle Pema, a Suopo local, knew the people and local situation quite well. At first, Mr. Chen and Uncle Pema wanted to appoint Teacher Dorje as the head. He was well connected with the county and had experience in tourism and knowledge of the queendom heritage, but Teacher Dorje declined the position because he thought it would be difficult to work with the "practical" Moluo villagers. Then Mr. Chen and Uncle Pema turned to Teacher Thubten, who enjoyed prestige in the village thanks to his uprightness and easygoing character and would be able to help the township manage tourism and "difficult" villagers in Moluo. He had the same concerns as Teacher Dorje, but Uncle Pema assured him that the position was temporary and someone else could take his place when everything was on the right track. Two village heads, the head of the village committee and the Party secretary of Moluo, and also the majority of seniors wanted him to take this post because they believed he was the only one who would be able to counteract Yeshe, who had expressed a strong desire for the position.

Yeshe ran for the post of village Party secretary in 2004 but did not win due to his negative image in the village. Although the head of the tourism association was not an official post, he was eager to take it, since it carried symbolic prestige and would give him a public stage for showcasing his talents and skills as a leader in front of "incompetent" village heads and suspicious villagers. Few wanted to give him such a chance, including the township Party secretary, Mr. Chen, as it was generally believed that Yeshe wanted to benefit only himself, not the whole village. His knowledge of Party policies, formidable eloquence, and confrontational style alienated him from Mr. Chen and other cadres who didn't want to have the Jiaju Gelindeya incident repeat itself in Moluo. But the township was aware that Yeshe's business acumen and creativity would contribute to tourism development in Moluo, so after negotiations among the seniors whom Uncle Pema had gathered, Yeshe was appointed vice-head. His role, however, was limited by the veto power of his superior, Teacher Thubten, and the presence of the other vice-head as well as the watchfulness of other members.

The rest of the association members were selected based on age, kinship ties, *guanxi*, literacy, and knowledge of local history and talents. Of the eight members, six were older than fifty because, according to Uncle Pema and others, in local tradition, old age itself demands respect and elderly people are considered more altruistic and devoted. Uncle Pema also attached great importance to kinship and *guanxi*. As China scholars point out, kinship ties were and are often a natural cause or source of political alliance or dissension in rural China,[7] and various forms of *guanxi* have also played an important part in reconfiguring social relations and power structures as well as remolding political goals and the interests of the actors concerned in socialist China (Mayfair Mei-Hui Yang 1994; Yan 1996). This is evident in Suopo, too: kinship ties and *guanxi* were a significant variable in deciding the tourism association's membership and shaping the power structure within it, since candidates with wider and stronger kinship ties and *guanxi* were expected to receive more support. As a result, all members except Yeshe share kin or *guanxi*, or both.

In Uncle Pema's view, since local culture and queendom traditions are major tourism resources in Moluo, the association must reserve seats for those with local knowledge. His son, a former monk, who is proficient in written Tibetan language and queendom legends and also good at singing folk songs and performing traditional dances, was recruited into the association. Uncle Pema argued that since entertainment was of essential importance in tourism, people with musical, artistic, and performing talents should be admitted, too. As a result, the association took in several who had such gifts. Besides Uncle Pema's son, who was in his early thirties, another man of similar age was also nominated due to his musical and performing skills. Of the eight members, only one is a woman, in her early fifties, who is very keen on singing and dancing.

In all, most of the candidates were nominated by Uncle Pema with the assistance of Teacher Dorje. They first reached consensus on the appropriate candidates and then persuaded some other seniors to nominate and vote for these candidates at the election meeting, which was attended by fourteen seniors and the two village heads. Next, the township gathered the Moluo villagers for a meeting, where a township cadre announced the names of the candidates and asked people to put up their hands if they approved of the slate of candidates. All attendees put up their hands as expected, so the nominations passed unanimously. Even if some villagers hadn't wanted to vote for certain candidates, they would have hesitated to vote against the group. Voting by raising hands instead of with secret ballots also discouraged villagers from expressing disagreement in public. Villagers were used to this kind of "democratic election" process from village elections,[8] so this procedure did not seem odd to them, and Uncle Pema's careful consideration of age, kinship, literacy, talents, and so on, seemed fair enough to most. In addition, many villagers didn't care much. The tourism association was a new concept for them, and they didn't fully understand what it was all about, nor did they expect much to change with its founding.

## THE ROLE AND AGENDAS OF THE TOURISM ASSOCIATION

The assumed purpose of establishing the tourism association was to let villagers manage their own tourism resources as a way of cultivating their sense of being responsible and qualified hosts for tourists, that is, hosts with "personal quality" (*suzhi*). The cadres like to say that the Suopowa "have very low personal quality" (*suzhi taidi*). This remark reflects countrywide anxiety over the issue of personal quality in Chinese national discourse, in which China's "low-quality" population, especially the peasants, are viewed by the Party-state and urban intellectuals as impediments to China's modernity and ascension to world power (Anagnost 2004). Many scholars point out that the Chinese state looks at tourism as a modern force that will transform its "backward" and "uncivilized" populations, especially minorities in remote regions with less access to "modern ideas."[9] Therefore, the Moluo

Tourism Association is expected to implement the state agenda of improving the personal quality of villagers in their interactions with tourists.

For Danba and Suopo cadres, "low personal quality" involves lack of both literacy and civility, concepts that overlap and usually are indistinguishable from each other. It is normally assumed that literate people possess civility, and vice versa. "Literacy" is a delicate concept in Suopo as in many other Tibetan regions, while the term "civility" (*wenming*) is widely applied throughout China, referring to proper manners and speech as well as attention to sanitary conditions. People with a traditional Tibetan education are often not counted by the state or by villagers themselves as literate or literate enough. Uncle Pema's son, a member of the tourism association, often referred to himself as "illiterate," although, as a former monk, he studied Tibetan scripture for some ten years. The idea of "literacy" thus centers upon proficiency in Chinese and the cultivation of proper manners inculcated through the Chinese education system. It also demonstrates that, to some extent, some local Tibetans have internalized the dominant state-imposed structure and discourse that has marginalized traditional means of education or non-Chinese education.

Villagers are supposed to learn to use such polite words as "thank you" and "please" and avoid rough and dirty words. Many locals don't bathe or change their clothes often, and some do not clean their houses regularly and are often accused by cadres of having a poor sense of sanitation. Because excrement from pigs, oxen, sheep, goats, and other livestock is visible in Moluo, the county and township governments often feel embarrassed in front of visitors and tourists. An important task of the tourism association is therefore to prod villagers into positive change through propaganda and education.

The tourism association is also expected to suggest to village heads and the township concrete means of developing tourism and disciplining villagers in their interactions with tourists. The township government underscored the importance attached to the tourism association by allocating a room to the association in the newly completed office building for Moluo's village committee. Most members, however, didn't really have any idea of how to proceed. Toward the end of 2008, the township heads, the Party secretary, and the newly appointed township head took the tourism association members to Jiaju to learn from the latter's tourism experiences. The Moluo visitors were impressed with Jiaju's cleanliness, the local guides' standard Chinese and eloquence, the villagers' "professional" manners, and the hospitality of tourist reception households. They also had the chance to listen to the former heads of the Jiaju Tourism Association, Bao and Zheng, talk about their experiences. Perhaps because of the presence of the Suopo cadres, Bao and Zheng talked as if the tourism association at Jiaju were still functioning, and they admonished the Suopo visitors that preserving cultural heritage and exhibiting "authentic" local culture to tourists were crucial to the success of tourism development, since tourists came to see the essence of traditional local Tibetan culture, not "modern" stuff. Both expressed admiration for Suopo's distinctive queendom cultural heritage. Bao, who held the post of the Party secretary of Suopo Township in the 1980s, even asserted that Suopo, with its queendom heritage, had much greater potential in the tourist market in China and even in the world.

The members of the Moluo Tourism Association read Mr. Bao's remarks as a reaffirmation of their cultural traditions. Like Bao and Zeng, most of these members were aware of the importance of cultural heritage as a tourist attraction. As Uncle Pema pointed out, both cultural learning and entertainment are important in tourism, so a healthy way of developing tourism in Suopo and Moluo is to combine the two by entertaining tourists with "real" culture. The tourism association shared this concern and decided to set up a *kordro* (a circle dance popular among Tibetans and other ethnic groups) troupe, a *bashe* (another kind of circle dance popular in the Kham region) troupe, and a folk-music band. The association encouraged villager participation, promising that they would eventually benefit economically when tourists came and paid for performances. This way of presenting or commercializing local culture had much to do with Yeshe. Every time the tourism association members met, he pushed his agenda of turning local resources into capital, indicating his disappointment with the incapacity, lack of imagination, and indifference of the local authorities. He insisted that the market was the only solution. He suggested inviting interested individuals and corporations from elsewhere in China to invest in Moluo, with the tourism association coordinating interactions with local authorities and villagers. The local authorities would play a smaller role in this ambitious project, and their interference with Moluo's tourism agendas would be undesirable. Not everyone agreed with him. Proponents of the cooperative position expected direction and financial as well as policy endorsements from the local authorities and preferred a safe and conventional development mode. No one could say that Yeshe was wrong, however, because of his success in business. Yeshe was frustrated with his "conservative" colleagues who were unable to understand his "modern" marketing plan and sometimes expressed the desire to quit.

As mentioned, it was Uncle Pema who charted the membership of the Moluo Tourism Association on behalf of the township government, and the Party secretary also made him assist the township head in overseeing the association's activities. Therefore, Uncle Pema's role in this association is significant. As the "King of the Eastern Queendom," he spares no effort in promoting the queendom cause and expects that the major task of the tourism association is to thoroughly investigate and revive the culture of the ancient queendom. He has been collecting legends on the queens for years and has made every effort to integrate the local oral history of the queendom with related Chinese and Tibetan historical records and literary writings in order to reconstruct the history of the Eastern Queendom. Due to his illiteracy in Tibetan, the evidence he cited for the existence of the queendom and its connection to Suopo was based almost exclusively on his reading of Chinese literature. He is fully aware of this shortcoming, and, to compensate, he often consulted his son, a former monk, and others who knew written Tibetan on the meanings of place-names and expressions that he assumed were associated with the queendom.

In 2008, a new graduate, originally from Suopo, who had studied Tibetan at college, got a position in Suopo Township. Uncle Pema took the opportunity to educate this young man about the importance of preserving queendom traditions and converted him to the queendom cause. One cadre in the township joked about their relationship, referring to the new employee as Uncle Pema's "disciple," who, like Uncle Pema, was not interested in administrative affairs and was concerned only with studying and promoting the queendom. Uncle Pema began learning "standard" Tibetan from this man, and I was impressed with his creative use of his limited Tibetan-language skills in the service of his goals. For instance, he argued that the Tibetan name of the Dadu River, which literally means "sweat of the queen," actually means "the river in front of the queen['s palace in Suopo]." In his view, since this river starts right in Suopo after its two major streams converge, the name itself is informative and symbolic: it tells the exact location of the queendom palace. Both his son and his Tibetan-language teacher commented that he would interpret many place-names or historical accounts imaginatively despite their corrections and protests.

The township Party secretary asked Uncle Pema to write a tour guide's speech for the tourism association that local guides could use as a standard introduction to local conditions and culture. He consulted me on how to write a vivid speech that would attract the attention of tourists as I had been a part-time tour guide. As one might expect, the speech was exclusively about queendom legends and claimed that only Suopo could be the site of the queens' palace. With the Party secretary's instructions, he and the young cadre who taught him written Tibetan also worked on packaging the ancient trees in Moluo for tourists. The Party secretary suggested that trees with unusual shapes should be packaged as tourist attractions by giving them exotic names related to the queendom. For instance, a certain tree could be dubbed "Queen's Horse-Tethering Tree" or "Queen's Reposing Tree." Since Uncle Pema is the authority on queendom issues, he was entrusted with embellishing the trees in Moluo with queendom cultural decorations.

Both the tour guide's speech and the tree-packaging project were authorized by the Party secretary and the township head in an attempt to orient and engage the Moluo Tourism Association in the mission of making concrete plans for developing tourism in Moluo. Some tourism association members admitted that they haven't done many "real" things yet. The association's ambiguous role often left its members puzzled about what they were supposed to accomplish. The principal task of the tourism association is to assist the township government and the village committee as well as the Culture and Tourism Bureau in coordinating the villagers' efforts to participate in and contribute to tourism development in Moluo. However, the actual responsibilities and functions of the tourism association were not clearly defined. This created a paradoxical impression of the position and role of the tourism association: on the one hand, it seemed that the association could do anything to promote tourism in Moluo as long as it didn't challenge the hegemonic role of the township government and the village committee; on the other hand, the association seemed powerless to implement plans since its activities were overseen and checked by the authorities.

From 2004 to 2007, the tension between Moluo villagers and the township on the distribution of tourist entrance fees was heating up, and in May 2007, a few tourists complained to the prefecture about the poor attitude of township cadres who were collecting entrance fees at the Suopo Bridge. Realizing how difficult it was to manage the villagers and deal with the tourists directly, the township government hoped that the tourism association would help ease this difficult situation. The tourism association members and some villagers believed that this was a "trick" and the township just wanted to shift its responsibilities and burdens to the association. Some, however, saw it as a signal from the township that the tourism association should resolve the trouble on its own. Since the township had also designated the membership, it seemed that the association could be fully entrusted with resolving these issues for the township. However, tourism association members complained that they were not given power or money to carry out their duties and that their real job was to "offend people," since disciplining the villagers and educating them about the proper behavior for soliciting tourism would provoke resentment.

The tension between the two camps paralyzed the tourism association. Although every member recognized Yeshe's creativity and business talent, most didn't trust him. They would not allow him to restructure the agenda in Moluo as he wished. His idea of corporatizing tourism by bringing in interested partners from all over China to manage tourism was simply too unconventional for most of the other members of the association and the villagers, and they had serious doubts about his "real" motives. Opposition from the association, villagers, and the township meant that there was little chance he would be able to realize his ambitious plans. Only one of the eight members supported him. According to this person, the other members' main agenda was to stop Yeshe from succeeding rather than to make concerted efforts so that the association would work. He sighed, "If the situation continues in this way, the tourism association will soon close down." This member had a personal connection with Yeshe, but he argued that it was not important at all in his judgment of Yeshe's character. He truly appreciated Yeshe's business gifts and believed that Yeshe was the only one who could lead Moluo in the right direction. In his opinion, what made Yeshe stand out from the "conservative" members and common villagers were his modern and innovative ideas, which they found unacceptable. According to this member, the villagers just wanted to make "small money" in the conventional way and had no idea of how the market worked. So, hindered by this strong conservative force, Yeshe could not apply his "advanced" ideas. This member blamed his fellow villagers for being "stupid" and not realizing that by preventing Yeshe from taking a more active role in the tourism association, they were harming only themselves, because without tourism development, he would still be the wealthiest man in the village. If they followed his advice instead, everyone would benefit eventually from the reinvigoration of tourism in Moluo.

This inaction on the part of the tourism association coincided with a slowdown in tourism in Danba during 2008 and 2009. Tourism had been seriously affected by the Tibetan riots in March 2008 and the Sichuan earthquake in May 2008. Although no uprising took place in Danba, and most of the locals, like their Han compatriots, condemned the Tibetan rebels for demanding independence, many potential tourists still imagined that Danba was a dangerous place to visit, since most of them were unable to distinguish between "rebellious" and "peaceful" Tibetans as a result of widespread Tibetophobia in China. At the same time, even though Danba was not severely affected by the earthquake, potential tourists from other parts of China still hesitated to explore it because of safety concerns. In the so-called Golden Week of October in 2008—the countrywide seven-day break for National Day—Moluo received only about a hundred tourists, and the tourism association collected just ¥1,088 ($159) in entrance fees. One villager commented:

> During the Golden Weeks in 2004, 2005, and 2006, we received so many tourists every day—as many as the ants. It was just like at the county seat. The path from the bridge to Moluo got so congested that it was almost impossible to get through. Last year, it was not bad. One or two thousand people came. This year, it was really horrible. The tourism association said it would distribute the money to each household. We have more than fifty households, so each one can get . . . how much? . . . A little over ¥10. I feel ashamed of accepting this money. What can such a small amount be used for? Buy a bag of salt? Haha.

The slowdown in Suopo continues through the writing of this book in 2012. It is a complicated matter involving many factors—the construction of a viewpoint platform on the highway from which tourists may look at the Suopo landscape and watchtowers for free, the non-operation of the newly completed Suopo Bridge, the county's tourism development agenda, which favors Jiaju and Zhonglu, and poor highway conditions from Chengdu to Danba. The lack of tourists contributed to the less active role of the tourism association. The association was expected to deal with problems in the locals' interactions with tourists, but since not many tourists came, there was little conflict, and the association did not seem to be doing anything real in the eyes of some villagers.

Several tourism association members reminded me that the association was "just a temporary phenomenon" and would complete its mission when tourism in Moluo and Suopo developed to the level of Jiaju. They argued that when tourism in Moluo and Suopo was standardized and the personal quality of locals improved, the association's original role of mediating and coordinating between tourists and villagers and between villagers and the township and county would diminish to the extent that it would become unnecessary. This idea originated with the newly elected township head, who used to be the vice-head of Niega Township (to which Jiaju belongs) in charge of tourism development in Jiaju. He took the post in Niega right after the Gelindeya incident, when Jiaju's tourism association was unofficially disbanded. His view of the destiny of the tourism association represents the official voice of the local state. When the county transferred him to the new post in Suopo, he began to publicize this ideology. Surprisingly (or maybe not), most of the Moluo Tourism Association members accepted this assertion, an indication of their lack of interest in engaging with the villagers in tourism development. They felt they didn't have enough resources to publicize Moluo and motivate villagers to participate, and they were aware that the villagers were difficult to deal with when conflicts arose. Their acceptance of the township head's opinion thus reflected their own uncertain and pessimistic attitude toward the future of the tourism association.

Jiaju's success in the tourism market is often used as an inspiring model for Suopo by both its township cadres and its tourism association members. It generated a belief that Jiaju's today is Suopo's tomorrow, and that Suopo, with its unique queendom heritage and cultural features, can catch up with and even outdo Jiaju. However, whether the experiences of the Jiaju Tourism Association could also serve as a model was unclear. The heads of Suopo Township took the Moluo Tourism Association members to Jiaju to learn "advanced" techniques from the former heads of its tourism association, even though the Jiaju Tourism Association had been unofficially dissolved. It was as if the Gelindeya incident had never happened. As the new head of Suopo Township and former vice-head of Niega claimed, since tourism at Jiaju had reached the mature stage and villagers were experienced and civilized enough to do the right things, the tourism association was no longer necessary. However, most members of the Moluo Tourism Association knew what had really happened to the Jiaju Tourism Association. Its demise reminded them of the limits of their role and subsequent counterstrategy: a safe role is the one that highlights their subordinate status vis-à-vis the village committee and the township.

### BEYOND STATE AGENDAS

In spite of the fact that Yeshe is a headache to the village and township, most members of the tourism association, especially Teacher Dorje and Teacher Namkha, are on good terms with the village heads and township cadres. The tourism association's allegiance to the authorities seems unchallenged, but this doesn't mean that the association is a mouthpiece of the local state. All members, including Yeshe, know exactly the importance of official support for their work. If they don't cooperate with the local authorities, their actions could be restrained, checked, or even invalidated, as was the case in Jiaju. They classify the tourism association as a grassroots association under the direct leadership of the village committee and township government. However, rather than always acting as the local authorities expected, the association became a public arena for the expression of different, even oppositional opinions as well as concerns about the queendom cause and vanishing cultural traditions.

A common topic of discussion among tourism association members was the county's unfair treatment and the status quo of the queendom cause. They unanimously attacked county officials for neglecting Suopo and declared that they would find their own way of rejuvenating and promoting their township. Several members expressed the following opinions:

> Zhonglu said that the queendom was in their place. What evidence have they got so far? They are lying. Several Zhonglu officials at the county seat even want to take away our queendom label? No way!

> If the tourism bureau doesn't promote tourism for us, we will do it by ourselves without their involvement. . . . There used to be so much publicity about Suopo, especially during the period when the Tibetan stone watchtowers were competing for World Cultural Heritage designation, but now what happened? . . . We must make use of our own excellent local

personnel to promote ourselves. . . . We have such rich cultural resources to excavate—Eastern Queendom culture, farm-plowing culture. . . . They are all our intangible cultural heritage [*feiwuzhi wenhua yichan*].

This year [2008] the county is not advertising our stone watchtowers. . . . The officials have almost forgotten our place. . . . Not many tourists are attracted here, but if you can help us invite some experienced experts to package Moluo, it will be a great boost to our work.

Some [village heads] lack a sense of responsibility. At first they seemed to be eager to see the results [of developing tourism ]. But tourism couldn't bring about immediate benefits [as they expected]. Then in the end, they didn't show much interest.

The county always criticizes us for being filthy, disorderly, and indecent [*zang, luan, cha*]. This is a typical example of subjectivism [*zhuguan zhuyi*]. . . . The famers have to raise livestock [and the animals excrete]. If they want cleanliness, too, how can they survive? They have to rely on the brown fields for a living.

We are renowned for the label "One-Thousand-Watchtower Kingdom" [Qiandiao Zhiguo], but we [Suopo] have become the largest garbage dumping site in Danba. The county built a garbage disposal site opposite our temple. From time to time, they would burn the garbage. It was so foul smelling that some women even fainted.

These remarks express dissatisfaction toward local officials for what are deemed to be nepotism, subjectivism, irresponsibility, dereliction of duty, and shortsightedness, but at the same time, tourism association members sought opportunities to change the status quo based on their sincere conviction that their queendom heritage and other cultural entities in Moluo and Suopo are truly exceptional and unrivaled. As mentioned, Yeshe would like to sell his idea of corporatizing Moluo. One proposal is that management be left to investors and each household would become a shareholder; the other scheme suggests welcoming other kinds of partnerships with interested individuals and groups. Although Yeshe's plans were too radical for most people, his insightful ideas on stimulating tourism in Moluo had an impact on the tourism association and the villagers. For instance, his suggestion that they rediscover queendom traditions, folk songs, and customs and establish a museum to exhibit traditional farming tools was well received by other members of the tourism association and some villagers. Although other association members take pride in the queendom heritage and attach importance to preserving vanishing cultural traditions, Yeshe is one of the few who knows how to turn queendom traditions and other cultural resources into commodities. For reasons already specified, it is difficult or nearly impossible for all of Yeshe's plans, especially the unconventional one of corporatizing Moluo, to be carried out in reality, but his strong presence as the most successful businessman and resourceful individual in the village and township solidifies his position at the tourism association.

Tourism association members often make use of *guanxi* in implementing their agendas.[10] One member made his brother-in-law's friend, the vice-head of the Culture and Tourism Bureau, promise at a new year's party where both got drunk to give the association ¥15,000 in "activities fees" (*huo-dongfei*) to fund its folk music and dance development project. Although this funding was from an official source, the association didn't obtain it through the regular process of requests and petitions. A former student of Teacher Dorje's, a department chair at a university who initiated several cultural preservation programs in Danba County, entrusted Teacher Dorje and Teacher Thubten with collecting disappearing folk songs and legends and donated ¥30,000 to build an activity center for the elderly and children in Moluo Village, which was in the charge of Teacher Dorje. Unlike other villages, where grassroots "seniors associations" (*laonian xiehui*) operate under the supervision of the county and township governments,[11] Moluo doesn't have such an association yet; however, the tourism association fulfills this role, as most of its members are respected village seniors.

As a result, the tourism association was given the activity center project with the approval of the township government and the village committee. After discussions among the members, the association selected a site right in front of the Berotsana pagoda, based on both practical and symbolic considerations.[12] With the increase in population, land has become more valuable and hard to obtain, but this small plot in the pagoda compound wasn't privately owned and thus could be used for the center. And since the pagoda compound is the ritual, religious, and social center of Moluo Village, Teacher Dorje and other members expected that the activities center would also serve as an educational center, which would pass on traditional culture and religious values to the younger generation, and a cultural museum, where tourists could catch a glimpse of the richness and unique-ness of local culture and the queendom traditions.

The Moluo Tourism Association may be seen as a "state-led civil society" (Frolic 1997), as its membership and agendas exhibit the strong organiza-tional will of Suopo Township.[13] The association is expected to assist the township in managing difficult villagers and is allowed to come up with its own tourism development agenda consistent with that of the township. The township does not want to see villagers incited to take action against the township and county, as occurred in Jiaju. The township Party secretary therefore appointed eight tourism association members at the suggestion of his subordinate, Uncle Pema. He also admitted Yeshe into the association due to Yeshe's business talents and connections. The wide acceptance among tourism association members of the new township head's claim that the association is just a temporary phenomenon best exemplifies the imprint of the state's will. Although most members take a cooperative position vis-à-vis the township, the association managed to carve out a space for express-ing negative opinions toward local authorities, pursuing the queendom cause, and implementing its own agendas.

The relationship between the tourism association and the township shows that it would be simplistic to dichotomize the state-society relation-ship or stress the hegemonic role of the Chinese state and the resistance/passivity of societal sectors.[14] The Moluo Tourism Association is both a quasi–state agency and a quasi–civil society. It is authorized and regulated by the local state but plays a role in connecting the local society and the state and in creating free space in which marginalized townspeople can voice grievances and press various political claims. State-society relations in Danba, as in China, should be seen as dynamic and multivalent. The differ-ing positions of the eight tourism association members regarding the asso-ciation's relationship with the local state, the existence of two camps representing divergent interests and mutual grudges, and the contrast between "conventional" and "modern" development models demonstrate that society itself is internally differentiated and is composed of sectors or individuals with different goals and concerns.

# CONCLUSION

*

The Suopowa are ethnically Zangzu, but they, along with other Gyarongwa, are marginalized by many other Zangzu, who claim that the Gyarongwa speak non-Tibetan languages/dialects and/or are culturally close to the Han. The Suopowa are unique among subgroups of Gyarong, as they speak a Khampa dialect, which they claim to be solid evidence of their "authentic" Tibetan origin in comparison to other Gyarongwa of "impure blood." However, other Khampa people do not usually count the Suopowa's language as Tibetan because they have difficulty communicating in that dialect. The Suopowa's belief in the Tibetan indigenous religion—Bon—has also often placed them in a disadvantaged position in respect to Tibetanness as conceived by the dominant Tibetan Buddhists. As a result, the Suopowa have developed a Tibetan identity that is insecure but also flexible and open. In response to their marginalized status in the Zangzu family, they have appropriated the image of the Eastern Queendom to highlight their unique status among Zangzu and in China. The Suopowa's queendom discourse also derives from their politically marginalized status in Danba. Accusing the county of practicing favoritism and nepotism, the Suopowa represent themselves as neglected townspeople. This self-representation is instrumental in pressing their queendom and other claims, since the assertion of marginality justifies their struggle for the queendom label and other political rights and benefits.

The Suopowa's queendom struggle encompasses local (i.e., Suopo Township and Danba County) sociopolitical and cultural contexts, the political marginality of the Suopowa, Zangzu identity and the Gyarongwa marginality, China's ethnic and Zangzu politics, ethnic representations in China, the lure of tourism, China's political reforms and social transformations, rural politics and grassroots unrest, and changing state-society interactions, as well as the Suopowa's responses to these situations and their self-representations. Therefore, the Suopowa's queendom struggle delineates a complex picture in which marginalities, real or imagined, inform and shape their multiple identities. Their modernist pursuit of a better politics and a better life as Danba inhabitants, as the Gyarongwa and Tibetans, as citizens and peasants of China, and also as objects of tourist exoticization and consumption demonstrates that treating them as marginalized or rebellious minority members, or as provincial and inward-looking peasants in an out-of-the-way place, obscures the intricacy and broader implications of the queendom discourse.

## THE CONVOLUTED LANDSCAPE
## OF THE QUEENDOM DISCOURSE

Who and what are the Suopowa? This seemingly simple question has no single, easy answer. The Suopowa's queendom discourse not only reflects the particular ethnic, cultural, and social contexts of the local society but also involves a much broader macroscopic environment—China's political transition, modernization agendas, rural reforms and grassroots unrest, ethnic representations, and Zangzu and minority politics. Therefore, the category "Suopowa" has different connotations in these different sociopolitical settings and embodies actors' dissimilar roles, responses, and identities in various contexts. Accordingly, the queendom discourse unpacks itself in each of these situations.

First, the term "Suopowa" refers to the residents of Suopo Township. The queendom struggle is rooted in this collective's common interests vis-à-vis those of other townships, especially their closest competitor, Zhonglu. Their shared destiny as bullied and marginalized townspeople in Danba County serves as an in-group and out-group boundary marker. Thus, people with different social backgrounds, agendas, and statuses are united against Zhonglu "thieves," other rivals (e.g., Jiaju), and especially the county in defense of their collective rights. The Han-Zangzu distinction is ignored in this context, and Dongfengwa, or the Han Gang, are considered the outer layer of the Suopowa category. Although the Suopowa are officially recognized members of the Tibetan ethnic group, their insecure Tibetan identity has prompted their desire to shun or drop the connection with Gyarong and accentuate their indispensable status among Tibetans through the queendom discourse.

As Chinese citizens, the Suopowa also congratulate themselves on the achievements of the Chinese government in combating poverty, improving living conditions for millions, and elevating China to the position of a formidable world power. They also declare their political allegiance to the Party by blaming Tibetan rioters for disturbing social stability and harming the common interests of the Zangzu public. Therefore, they assume that their political rights should be safeguarded by the state, especially the powerful, "pure" central state, and have every confidence in justice and the success of their queendom and other political claims. Regardless of their Chinese citizenship, their minority status as Zangzu registers their difference from the Han and from other "peaceful" or less "colorful" minorities. As an ethnic minority in China, they are subject to China's ethnic politics and representations. Qualities popularly associated with Tibetans, such as primitiveness, masculinity, wildness, religiousness, simplicity, innocence, and rebelliousness, as well as China's ethnic policy, specifically toward Zangzu, inform and shape the Suopowa's self-representations. The queendom discourse is more than a political struggle against the "corrupt" local state; it is also a challenge to negative portrayals and a simultaneous justification and substantiation of local Tibetans' positive images in the Chinese official and popular discourses. They advocate this agenda through their announced allegiance to the Party-state as well as their assumed superior morality and civility. As expressed in the queendom discourse, only Suopo males know how to treat women properly on account of their self-presentation as real gentlemen and "authentic" men who are morally superior to the Han and other men in a male-chauvinist world that has unjustly rendered women subordinate to men.

Furthermore, as mountain peasants, the Suopowa, together with millions of Chinese peasants in other less developed provinces and regions, are often assumed by the state and urban population to have very low personal quality, as indicated by limited sanitation, low literacy, and "conservative" outlooks (e.g., clinging to "feudal" traditions such as male privilege, folk religious rituals, etc.). Therefore, Suopo must be modernized materially and spiritually by accommodating itself to rapid social transformations through such means as tourism development and implementation of the country-wide New Socialist Countryside Construction project. The queendom discourse is embedded in local responses to this modernist agenda and is inseparable from local anticipation of a profitable tourism industry and a modern way of life, and the Suopowa use various modern means such as the media and the Internet to promote their queendom agenda and tourism. The Suopowa also present an image of "civility," namely, high moral standards and women's status in local society, as a subtle challenge to the state's modern personal-quality discourse. The queendom struggle is an example of the rural unrest and peasants' collective action that have become common in China as a consequence of intensified reforms and the unprecedented sociopolitical transformation of rural society.

The complexity of the queendom discourse is also revealed through the internal heterogeneity of both Suopo societal sectors and the state as well as through dynamic ongoing state-society interactions. Even though Suopo is only a small administrative unit in Danba County, issues related to who are the real Suopowa and who are authentic descendants of the queens exhibit conspicuous village-based nepotism, various degrees of lineage and cultural purity in relation to the ancestral queens, crystallization of Han-Tibetan dissimilarities, and divergence of political goals. Elites and common villagers show different concerns and interests in the queendom dispute, and the Suopowa show varying degrees of awareness of the implications of negative or sexualized images associated with the queendom and local women. The members of the Moluo Tourism Association also have divergent opinions on the association's relationship with the township and on development models. These are, to some extent, an extension of everyday intravillage disagreements. Likewise, the state is far from being a homogeneous whole.

Many Suopowa speak highly of the "great" policies and "purity" of the Chinese central government while blaming local state officials for their irresponsibility or corruption even though the majority of county and township officials are Zangzu. This shows that the Suopowa don't see the state as a monolithic unit and that they have developed a hierarchical preference for different levels of the state, imagining that the closer a certain level of the bureaucracy is to the central state, the better and less corrupted it is. This also indicates that although the local state is in the hands of Zangzu, the Suopowa are inclined to judge the state based not on its ethnicity but on its performance, even if many locals are skeptical about Han practices and morality in general. In Suopo Township, four out of six officials are listed as Zangzu on their IDs. Most Suopowa don't have a clear idea about whether these four officials are "real" Zangzu or not.[1] At the county level, more than two-thirds of the leading officials are ethnically Zangzu, too—most Suopo locals neither know nor care about this. My Suopo informants declare that the ethnicity of these officials is not their concern, and what really matters is whether they take their work and the people seriously.

Suopo Township's ambivalent attitude toward the queendom dispute suggests that the township has its own agenda and interests. The township cadres' middle-way approach of neither expressing public support nor cutting the debate short is their most pragmatic choice, allowing them to avoid resentment from Suopo villagers and censure from county authorities. In similar fashion, the county government also takes an ambiguous attitude toward the queendom dispute. The Suopowa's claim has already been approved by an important leader from the prefecture; thus, county leaders chose not to dismiss the claim, but they do not endorse it, either. These cases indicate that although the Chinese state is known for its authoritarian and top-down ruling style, various levels of the local state have room for pursuing their own objectives and concerns or, at the very least, a chance to abdicate responsibility and let a situation play itself out more or less free of external intervention.

The way of engagement between the Moluo Tourism Association and the local state exemplifies the dynamic relationship between these two sectors. The tourism association is both a quasi–state agency, due to the penetration of state power and local state regulations, and a quasi–civil society, thanks to its role in linking local society with the local state and generating free space for political claims. Thus the relationship between the tourism association and local state is neither oppositional nor simply cooperative. It is a much more complex interrelation that needs to be contextualized and deconstructed.

The Suopowa's manipulation of their marginal status in China and among Zangzu contributes to the convolution of the queendom landscape. This tactic stems from their assessment of the power structure and overall situation that have placed them on the periphery. They have worked to turn the disadvantage of marginality into an advantage and find a proper niche for themselves in the existing social and political system.

## STRATEGIC MARGINALITY AND THE CONVERGENCE ZONE

The Suopowa are situated on the periphery in both the Chinese sociopolitical landscape and the Tibetan ethno-national terrain. Nevertheless, marginality need not constitute merely a constraint or circumscription that confines actors on the damned and dismal periphery; it can be an opportunity to act for benefits. The Suopowa not only take advantage of their marginal status for the vigorous promotion of their political goals but also advertise their assumed marginality with the anticipation of rewards and compensation.[2]

Marginality can be a rare resource in some situations. Although the Suopowa may be looked down upon by other Tibetans as "impure" or "fake" Tibetans, their linguistic, cultural, and historical distinctiveness can become an important source of attraction or pride. The multiplicity of magnificent stone watchtowers and the flourishing of the queendom heritage have elevated Suopo in the local discourse as an unmatched place in Zangzu regions and in China. The Suopowa take delight in the assumption that their stone watchtowers are probably the oldest and are among the most historically significant structures throughout Zangzu areas. Some of them, especially local elites, promote the intact queendom tradition of valuing women over men as evidence of their unrivaled nobleness and civility among Zangzu and in relation to the Han and others and propose that their religious marginality as Bon followers in a predominantly Tibetan Buddhist world illustrates their incomparable broad-mindedness and tolerance. As a result, the Suopowa have earned enough social capital to support their advertising of Suopo as a truly exceptional and touristically peerless destination in the Chinese tourist market.

The Suopowa also make use of their asserted political marginality in Danba as justification for their queendom struggle and other claims. The

Suopo Bridge and queendom issues are said to demonstrate the county's unfair treatment of them. A similar claim is made by people from Moluo Village, one of the first two villages in Danba selected in 2008 for the government-funded New Socialist Countryside Construction development project. Moluo is also the only village in Danba County that has been officially granted the prestigious and valuable label "Famous Historical and Cultural Village of China." Construction of the big new Suopo Bridge, which will allow buses and cars to enter Moluo, was initiated in 2008 and completed in 2011; a new road from the bridge to Moluo Village was finished in 2009 and will be extended to connect another six villages on the eastern bank of the Dadu River over the next few years. The county is also promoting Suopo's stone watchtowers to the media and tourists in the hope that this ancient architecture will be formally placed on the World Cultural Heritage list. If this does occur, Suopo, especially Moluo Village, is expected to become a more important tourist destination. Nonetheless, the Suopowa, including Moluo villagers, still loudly complain that they are treated "badly" by the county. How can one make sense of this?

To a large extent, this phenomenon originates in the bureaucratic dysfunctions and falsifications prevalent in the Chinese political system. Various government agencies in Danba—as in other Zangzu regions and all parts of China—prepare different statistics and reports on the same issue that are delivered to different departments of the higher state. When required to display their achievements, they will present a version of the statistics that shows progress. When they need to demonstrate their difficulties and harsh working conditions, they will present a different version, highlighting their tough situation and highly motivated working spirit. In doing so, local officials hope to receive financial support or preferential treatment from their superiors. Suopo villagers have learned this trick, too, knowing that if they complain to officials and outsiders, they may be compensated or rewarded later in one way or another. With the increasing investment and financial support available for the development of Zangzu and other regions in the past decade, this strategy has become increasingly common. They also hoped that outsiders like me, as well as other scholars or intellectuals, will help voice local grievances in a way that could pressure the county government so that the Suopowa could keep what they've gained and even improve their prospects.

Suopo males' self-feminization is another prominent case of strategic marginality, although this has a different focal point and evokes different impressions from that of political marginality. With political marginality, the Suopowa construct and publicize the pitiful image of townspeople who are unjustifiably neglected in Danba, while with self-feminization, local men design a somewhat atypical but desirable picture of women's queenly superiority in local society. In both cases, the Suopowa strategically choose to ignore or renounce the possibility of identifying with the dominant group or discourses, instead placing themselves on the far margin in exchange for benefits. An inevitable consequence of propagating the queen-dom discourse is that Suopo men have to abandon the symbolically domi-nant virile Khampa image—at least for the time being—and embrace an emasculated self-representation. This seemingly degrading act is not, how-ever, equal to the repudiation or sacrifice of their virility. On the contrary, it is a pronounced declaration of their unmatched manliness as evidenced by their recognition and advancement of women's status.

Although their marginal status may have brought the Suopowa various advantages, most of the time they claim to be either part of both the Han/state and the Tibetan centers or part of one or the other. The justification for this assertion has everything to do with the obscurity and ambiguity of their historical and cultural traits and hence ethnic identity. Just as they are able to foreground their difference, they have no difficulty underlining sameness and swearing allegiance to these two centers. The Suopowa approvingly identify with the central state and proclaim their legitimacy as Chinese citizens just as do the Han. They choose to centralize themselves as people who are as deserving of equal rights as the Han, but many Suo-powa believe that Tibetans, including themselves, are more "civilized" than the Han in general because of their religious beliefs and unique traditions. In contrast, the Han are often portrayed as money-hungry, dishonest, untrustworthy, and of comparatively lower moral standards. The Suopowa thus propagate their Tibetanness and highlight their Tibetan centrality, positioning themselves at the Tibetan core and placing the Dongfengwa at the margin. They authenticate this claim by specifically stressing their ancestral, linguistic, and cultural connections with the Tibetan mainstream while dismissing ambiguities.

Although the Suopowa have recognized the dominant position of both the Han and Tibetan centers and aligned themselves with these two centers, this alliance stems precisely from their political marginality in China as well as the ethno-national periphery of the pan-Tibetan or Zangzu identity. The Suopowa also endeavor to construct Gyarong and Suopo as another dynamic center. Gyarong was a relatively independent political and cultural entity vis-à-vis Tibetans and the Han before 1950. Despite the fact that Gyarong has been increasingly integrated into the Zangzu family and the Han/state since Liberation, its historical particularity, linguistic-cultural singularity, and sociopolitical specificity still inform a separate identity. Consequently, in local discourse, Gyarong constitutes a vital center in and for itself and thus interacts with both the Tibetan and Han centers as a relatively self-sufficient and autonomous political and cultural entity. The message conveyed in the queendom cause that the Suopowa are morally "superior" to other Tibetans, the Han, and even Westerners thanks to the claimed dominant position of women in the local society is not surprising. This is another example of the Suopowa's attempt to demonstrate their centrality, but rather than being a validation of closeness to Tibetan or Han centers, it is an unreserved demonstration of the Suopowa's supremacy and thus their attempt to set an example for both the Han and Tibetans.

The center and periphery are not absolute but are elastic, situational, negotiable, and even reversible in certain circumstances. Therefore, always placing the Suopowa on the periphery of the dominant Han and Tibetan realms is not justifiable. The Suopowa may in fact sometimes reverse this structure by placing the Han and other Tibetans on the margin instead. The notions of both hybridity (Bhabha 1994) and creolization (Hannerz 1992) spotlight this dialectic center-periphery paradigm, but their focus on the inherently "impure" and "bastard" quality of peripheral populations and cultures prevents them from fully depicting and grasping the distinctive identities of marginal societies and their capacity for counteracting the powerful centers. Therefore, the idea of a convergence zone is more useful for conceptualizing the Suopowa's dynamic interplay with the two centers and their effort to strategize their marginal status and centralize themselves as an independent party interacting with both centers.

In this convergence zone, the Suopowa can move relatively freely between the Han and the Tibetan centers or choose to safeguard their own social and cultural territory. Nevertheless, there is no absolute freedom in their choices and actions. Their decision is based on the evaluation of the status quo and available conditions. There is no way for them to display their centrality all the time. The ubiquitous presence of the Han/state and Tibetan influence makes it sensible for them to identify with these two centers, but this choice is not made by rationally assessing all possible consequences. Oftentimes the choice is influenced by historical and cultural bonds, and especially the state's ruling system and ethnic and Zangzu policies. Their alignment with the state and the Tibetan ethnic group doesn't necessarily originate from calculation of potential benefits and rewards; instead, it is inseparable from the ineradicable impacts of historical, political, and cultural convergences between the centers and local society and the subsequent attachment of the latter to the former. This situation illustrates the complications of a convergence zone.

In intensive encounters, interactions, competitions, or conflicts with powerful centers, a local society that acts as a convergence zone has absorbed various elements from dominant societies and cultures. Nevertheless, natives are not necessarily integrated into the centers, and in some circumstances, they even choose to escape from the state and other powerful sociopolitical entities, as is illustrated in James Scott's portrayal of the Zomian case (2009). In Zomia—an interstate zone linking a number of mostly Southeast Asian countries—people choose to become fugitives from the state and "modernity." Although the Suopowa have taken a different approach in their interactions with the state and "mainstream" Tibetans, from time to time, they may invoke their separate identity and even moral centrality in order to distinguish themselves from the Han and Tibetans. The idea of a convergence zone similarly illuminates the impacts and constraints of powerful centers as well as local agency in building local centrality.

Suopo, Danba, and Gyarong are not situated at the end of Tibetan or Han cultural and political territories but in the convergence zone where these two sociopolitical and cultural worlds encounter each other, contest, and converge, where local identities as the Suopowa, the Danbawa, and the Gyarongwa negotiate with their Tibetan identity, their relationship to the Han, and their status as Chinese citizens. It is a space where border ambiguity or marginality can be appropriated as a rare resource and opportunity. This convergence zone is characterized by dynamic interactions between sameness and difference as well as bursts of creativity and innovation that have emerged out of constant reconfigurations. Various degrees of sameness and difference in the Suopowa in relation to the Han and Tibetans have placed them in a unique context: they can claim both Tibetan identity and, like the Han, the identity of Chinese citizens, and they can also assert their distinctiveness, exclusivity, and superiority vis-à-vis both the Han and Tibetans. Thus, in Suopo, Danba, and Gyarong, we see not only how the Han and Tibetan worlds converge or hybridize but how an indigenous society on the borders encounters and negotiates with these two powerful sociopolitical and cultural centers as well as how a new people, identity, and center have been born out of these multiple convergences. Vicissitudes of individual and group variation also are evident within this contested and transformative space. The Suopowa's attempt to claim the queendom label exemplifies this complicated process. Through the lens of the queendom struggle, one can see personal, social, political, and cultural transformation and reconfigurations of Zangzu society as well as the multiple contradictions and ambivalences of Chinese society at the levels of both governmental and personal identity. Simultaneously, it is obvious that the Suopowa's responses to such changes are deeply rooted in their own local cultural and political contexts. The queendom discourse thus engenders and represents an unusually rich and nuanced sociopolitical landscape.

# NOTES

1    See Pratt 1991; Tsing 1993; Ortner 1999; Mueggler 2001.
2    See Hannerz 1992, 265. See also Korom 1994; Spitzer 2003.

## 1. SETTING FOOT IN THE QUEEN'S LAND

1    As has been pointed out by Janet Gyatso in "Down with the Demoness:
     Reflections on a Feminine Ground in Tibet," *Tibet Journal* 12(4): 38–53,
     some Western scholars have also identified the existence of probably two
     women's countries in an area bordering Tibet, based on both Chinese and
     Indian sources. See, for example, William Woodville Rockhill, *The Land
     of the Lamas* (London: Longmans, Green, and Co., 1891); Giuseppe Tucci,
     *Preliminary Report on Two Scientific Expeditions in Nepal* (Rome: Istituto
     Italiano per il Medio ed Estremo Oriente, 1956); Frederick William
     Thomas, *Ancient Folk-Literature from North-Eastern Tibet* (Berlin: Abhan-
     dlungen der Deutschen Akademie der Wissenschaften zu Berlin, 1957); and
     Rolf Alfred Stein, *Tibetan Civilization* (Stanford, CA: Stanford University
     Press, 1972). Erik Haarh, *The Yar-Lun Dynasty* (Copenhagen: GEC Gad's
     Forlag, 1969), and Thomas, *Ancient Folk-Literature from North-Eastern
     Tibet*, suggest that there were certain significant elements of women's lin-
     eage and even political dominance in ancient Tibet.

2    The *Book of Sui*, compiled in the seventh century, is the official history of
     the Sui dynasty (581–618). The *History of Northern Dynasties*, also compiled
     in the seventh century, covers the period 386–618. The *Old Tang History*,
     completed in the tenth century, is the earliest existing systematic historical
     record of the Tang dynasty (618–907). The *New Tang History*, compiled in
     the eleventh century, is a revised version of the *Old Tang History*.

3    See Xueniu 2003; Lin Junhua 2006a; Ma Chengfu 2006; Wang Huailin
     2006.

4    Gyarong extends to Hongyuan County (T: Khyung Mchu or Rka Khog
     Rdzong) in Aba Tibetan and Qiang Autonomous Prefecture (T: Rnga Ba
     Bod Rigs Dang Chang Rigs Rang Skyong Khul) to the north; Rangtang
     County (T: 'Dzam Thang Rdzong) in Aba prefecture and Seda County (T:
     Gser Rta Rdzong) in Ganzi Tibetan Autonomous Prefecture (T: Dkar
     Mdzes Bod Rigs Rang Skyong Khul) to the northwest; Luhuo County (T:
     Brag Mgo Rdzong) and Yajiang County (T: Nyag Chu Kha Rdzong) in
     Ganzi prefecture to the west; Mianning County in Liangshan Yi Autono-
     mous Prefecture to the south; Shimian County, Tianquan County, and
     Baoxing County of Ya'an City to the southeast; and Wenchuan County in
     Aba prefecture and Dujiangyan (City) of Chengdu City to the east.

5    The Gyarong region does not have a clearly defined border. The map shows
     a "broad" Gyarong or Gyarong in its historical context. Today, what people
     refer to as "Gyarong" is much smaller in size, and thus many places that
     may be part of Gyarong historically are no longer recognized as Gyarong
     by either local residents or the "authentic" Gyarongwa. As mentioned, the
     majority of the Gyarong region lies in today's Aba prefecture.

6    The *tusi* system was an administrative tactic applied to minority regions
     in northwestern, southwestern, and southern China. It started in the Mon-
     gols' Yuan dynasty (1271–1368), flourished in the Ming dynasty (1368–1644),
     and declined in the Manchus' Qing dynasty (1644–1911). Through confer-
     ring the *tusi* title upon the local chiefs, the imperial court ruled these
     regions indirectly through these officially recognized posts. At the same
     time, the *tusi* were obliged to pay tribute to the court, fulfilling certain
     political, economic, and military duties. According to Jia Xiaofeng (2007),
     in all Tibetan regions including Gyarong, there were 849 *tusi*, of whom 795,
     or roughly 94 percent, were Tibetans.

7    According to Quedan (1995), the total population of the Gyarongwa by 1995
     was 370,000. This number is questionable, since he seemed to count other
     Zangzu populations in this region as the Gyarongwa, too. So it suggests
     that in practice, the category of "Gyarongwa" is often ambiguous.

8   For instance, when the Gyarongwa meet with Tibetans in other regions and are asked about their origin, some Gyarongwa mention only the names of bigger places like Aba and Ganzi prefectures, since the popular impression of many Tibetans outside these two prefectures is that Aba prefecture is dominated by Amdo Tibetans and Ganzi prefecture by Khampa.

9   The consensus among historians is that ancient records on Gyarong in both Chinese and Tibetan are seriously lacking, so it is tremendously hard, if not impossible, to delineate a clear historical landscape of Gyarong.

10  See, e.g., Ma Changshou 1944; Li Shaoming 1980; Deng 1986; Gele 1988; Shi 2001; Guo Shengbo 2002; Yang and Yang 2004; Zeng 2004.

11  See Wang Yao 1987; Li Xingyou 1995; Btsan Lha 1999, 2004.

12  See Sun Hongkai 1983; Jackson Sun 2000; Jacques 2008.

13  Tea, yak butter, and *tsampa* often serve as the marker that defines essential Tibetanness. In my interactions with Tibetans all over the Tibetan regions, many emphasize that this food constitutes the essence of Tibetan identity. A popular belief is that other peoples—particularly Han—cannot get used to yak butter and *tsampa*. Therefore, sometimes Tibetan youth who don't consume much yak butter and *tsampa* are accused of being Sinicized. This is not the self-image only of "traditional" Tibetans, however; the Han and other peoples tend to associate this food with Tibetanness, too.

14  Wuhouci is a district with the largest number of Tibetan stores and restaurants in Chengdu City, which also has a large Tibetan population that is composed mainly of businessmen, salespeople, migrant workers, monks, college students, and other Tibetan visitors and tourists.

15  Since the late eighteenth century, more and more Han have immigrated to Gyarong. Today, the Gyarongwa and the Han live next to each other in many villages. The Gyarongwa have adopted substantial Han cultural elements such as various festivals. Han influence is now much more pronounced in language, food, education, popular culture, and everyday aspects of life. In terms of religious belief, some Gyarongwa also resort to Han Daoist priests due largely to the lack of great Tibetan priests and lamas. This has had a certain effect on Gyarongwa's religious and/or Tibetan identity. The place of the Han in Gyarong will be discussed in more detail in chapter 4 of this volume.

16  Some reincarnate lamas have a number of Han and Western followers, who have donated a great deal to these projects.

17  The following cases illustrate the influence a well-reputed lama can exert on a local community. In the first, a friend of mine who is a very learned

Gelugpa lama returned to his hometown several years ago with the prestigious *geshe* degree. Since his return, his influence in this region has been significant. For instance, he admonished locals not to accumulate bad karma by killing wild animals, and this activity has almost disappeared. I launched an opera revival project and a Tibetan-language training program through him because I knew that the villagers listen to him and would devote themselves to both if their beloved lama directed them to do so. No other lama from the local monastery has had such influence. All the other monks were trained in the same monastery, but on the whole they haven't acquired the same advanced knowledge of scripture and Buddhist philosophy. Another example is that locals in Suopo greatly respect a learned Bon lama for his sophisticated training in Bon and Tibetan medicine as well as his compassion for others. Sometimes the locals refer to him as the "reincarnate lama," although he is not formally recognized as such by any temple. According to one Suopo villager, this lama was a "real lama," different from most other monks who "don't know much." His kindness and compassion are also unparalleled in Suopo. This villager thus concluded, "If Suopowa don't want to do certain things, the township cadres cannot do anything about it. Even if the county head came, nothing would change. [However,] if he [this lama] says we should do it, then all of us will listen."

18  Samten Karmay (1996) also points out that the relatively harmonious relationship between Bon and Buddhism in Danba and Gyarong is rarely seen in Tibetan regions (1996).

19  UNESCO's World Heritage website describes the architecture as follows:

> The shapes of old Diaolou Buildings in Danba are diversified, with quadrangular, pentagonal, octagonal and tridecanal towers. The majority of them are quadrangular Diaolou Buildings. . . .
>
> The old watchtower takes up an area of 25~120 m², with a height varying from 10 to 60 m. Mountain rocks and slates, yellow mud and timber are adopted as the main building materials. With a relatively bigger base, the Diaolou Buildings narrow upward to the top. The towers were built with rocks and slates of various sizes. As many walls were built with rocks weighing over several hundred kilos, the walls prove firm, thick and solid. They are built with well-leveled surfaces and pointed corners, making the tower stand straight and upright. The function of the old Diaolou Buildings varies, combining military and residential purposes. They fall mainly into two categories: folk towers and residential towers. By

its own particular function, they can be further labeled as war flame tower, strategic pass tower, official village tower, boundary tower, scripture tower, and tower in houses, etc. The old Diaolou Buildings in Danba have survived wars, weather, and earthquakes. With a long history, they rise straight from the land, towering loftily, solid and strong as usual. Some of them stand as bows, forming quite marvelous spectacle, making one amazed at its refined and intricate arts of building. In 2006, the old Diaolou Buildings in Danba were enlisted as the Cultural Relics of National Importance by the State Department.

From "Diaolou Buildings and Villages for Tibetan and Qiang Ethnic Groups," UNESCO, http://whc.unesco.org/en/tentativelists/5343/. Accessed 2009.

### 2. MASCULINE AND FEMININE INTERNAL OTHERS IN CHINA

1   See, e.g., Stoler 1989; Sinha 1995; Young 1995; Cooper and Stoler 1997; Catherine Hall 2000; Nagel 2003.
2   See Spence 1981; Kinkley 1987; Oakes 2007.
3   See Ding Chunlian 2002; Li and Huang 2004; Han 2007; Wang Haiying 2007; Wu Wenyu 2008.
4   See Tobin, Wu, and Davidson 1989; Wang Xianhua 2003; Liang, Li, and Huang 2006.
5   However, the popular conception often makes a distinction between urban and rural boys. Usually urban boys are said to be much softer than rural ones, since the country boys, especially those from poverty-stricken or mountainous regions, are able to "eat bitterness" (*chiku*), meaning they develop the capacity to endure difficulties, thereby engendering strong and virile personalities.
6   This phrase is often used to identify bookish and effete male students and scholars who become "pallid-faced" because of the lack of outdoor physical exercise.
7   Sinha 1995; Clancy-Smith and Gouda 1998; Catherine Hall 2000; Nagel 2003; Ghosh 2004; Teng 2004; Ballantyne and Burton 2005.
8   For instance, Western-educated, middle-class Bengali Hindu males were depicted as the opposite of manly and chivalrous Englishmen and were believed to be "effeminate, bookish, over-serious, languorous, lustful and lacking in self-discipline" (John MacKenzie, quoted in Sinha 1995, vii). Its ultimate purpose was to spotlight the exclusive privilege of the Britons in

India: "the charge of 'effeminacy' to isolate certain native groups check-mated the demand to extend political rights to Indians; and the 'unnatu-ralness' in the claims for political and legal equality of these groups extended the rationale for continued Anglo-Indian racial domination" (Sinha 1995, 63). As a result, British prerogatives and "inalienable" rights as the chosen people were legitimized and fortified as being for the Indians' good. In other words, the damned status of Indians was determined by their own incompetency and effeminacy, which necessitated the colonial rule of the powerful and benevolent British Empire, which "took great troubles" to "take care of" them.

9    See Gladney 1991; Litzinger 2000; Schein 2000; Harrell 1995, 2001.

10   The rulers of the last Chinese dynastic empire, the Qing, were Manchu, but they spared no effort in promoting Confucian ideals and modeled them-selves after the court system, ruling practices, and political doctrines of the Han-based Ming dynasty. From the very beginning, the Qing rulers looked up to the Han culture and adopted assimilation policies by and for them-selves, thus legitimizing their claim to being the true holders and defenders of Chinese culture. Toward the end of the nineteenth and the beginning of the twentieth century, Manchu rulers were very much Sinicized. So together with the Han, in some ways the Manchus were also civilizers who occupied the center of the "central kingdom" and carried out the "civiliz-ing project" to moralize or "humanize" other minorities. Like the Manchus, some other peoples, such as the Naxi and the Bai, were on the list of the most "civilized" and Sinicized minorities.

11   The term "strange barbarians" refers to those whose cultural practices are still very "primitive" and distant from the Han civilization, while "familiar barbarians" describes peoples who are much more Sinicized and thus more "civilized." The same minority group may be subdivided into "strange" and "familiar" as well, depending on how much they were integrated into the Chinese culture. For instance, Miao in southern and southwestern China were classified as either "familiar" or "strange": "familiar Miao" lived closer to Han settlements in sedentary communities where they were under some kind of governance, paid taxes, did corvée labor, and mani-fested a modicum of Chinese cultural influence; "strange Miao" were unruled, paid no taxes, were not required to perform service, and lived in terrain that, from the Han point of view, was more rugged and isolated (Schein 2000, 7).

12   At first, more than four hundred groups self-registered as independent ethnic groups, but only fifty-six ethnic groups including the Han were

recognized. The criteria for identification were based on Stalin's four "golden rules"—"a common language, a common territory, a common economic life, and a common psychological make-up manifested in common specific features of national culture" (Gladney 1991, 66).

13 According to Chuan-Kang Shih, toward the end of the Cultural Revolution, a dramatic campaign against "primitive" walking marriage, the One-Wife-One-Husband Movement, was launched to force sexual partners to get married. As a result, 424 couples in the Yongning area were forced into registered marriages (Shih 2010, 4).

14 See Wagner 1975; MacCannell 1976; Hanson 1989; Linnekin 1990; Dietler 1994; Hobsbawm 1994; Lindholm 2008.

15 See, e.g., Louie 2002; Khan 1996; Hillman and Henfry 2006.

16 The search for romantic encounters has become a significant component of ethnic tourism in many parts of the world and has engendered a number of internationally acclaimed ethnosexual tourism destinations such as Thailand, the Philippines, Sri Lanka, Belize, Jamaica, Brazil, Costa Rica, Cuba, and Kenya (see, e.g., Graburn 1983; Truong 1990; C. M. Hall 1994; Pruitt and LaFont 1995; Ryan and Kinder 1996; Enloe 2000; Ryan and Hall 2001). Male and female sex workers use their ethnic bodies to satisfy the tourists' desires for authentic sexual experiences, which may be scarce back home.

17 The Mosuo have a population of about forty thousand, live on the southeastern fringe of the Tibetan Plateau, and speak a Tibeto-Burman language. Mosuo territory straddles the border of Yunnan and Sichuan provinces and includes Ninglang, Muli, Yanyuan, and Yanbian Counties. One of its primary geographical features is Lugu Lake. Promoted as the cultural center of Mosuo territory, Lugu Lake has become a major tourist attraction in northwestern Yunnan. The Chinese government does not recognize the Mosuo as an ethnic group; instead, it officially classifies the Mosuo in Yunnan as a subgroup of the Naxizu and those in Sichuan as Mongolian. In the late 1980s, the Mosuo's attempts to gain state recognition won them the right to call themselves "Mosuo people" (*Mosuo ren*). The Mosuo practice Bon and Tibetan Buddhism as well as dabaism, their own form of shamanism. Before 1956, the *tusi*, or local chiefs or kings, had controlled the area for more than six hundred years (Walsh 2005, 451–52).

18 Many female tourists are eager to find out what is going on there. Some are drawn by the appeal of Mosuo men, who are also romanticized as "great lovers."

19 However, as Eileen Rose Walsh points out, many of these popular repre-

sentations of the Mosuo are not true. According to her, in the rural villages of Yongning Township, Ninglang County, Yunnan, almost one-third of households are headed by males, and even in the households with women as heads, major decisions concerning property are often made by the senior or most economically productive man (Walsh 2005, 453). In love relations, control by women is exaggerated. Both women and men exercise autonomy in their mutual relations. Men can choose to stay or terminate their relationships, as can women. Moreover, the relative autonomy of both women and men in selecting partners is not equal to free love, which has the connotation of promiscuity, a concept imposed by ethnocentric outsiders. Locals have their own principles and rules for this kind of relationship (see Cai Hua 2001, 231–32, 251–52), and furthermore, other modalities of sexual life, such as cohabitation and marriage, do exist in this society. As for the enviable familial harmony, discord and disputes among family members do occur, as in other societies, and thus sometimes separation is unavoidable (see, e.g., ibid, 160–64). With the increase in tourism, tensions among villagers, between different villages, and between villagers and the government have become common due to competition, asymmetrical wealth distribution, and different agendas for tourism development, as will be seen in the parallel cases of Suopo and Danba.

20   Tami Blumenfield (2010) delineates a very nuanced picture of how Mosuo people and practices are represented in the media, not only from the outside but also from within by locals themselves.

## 3. FROM THE VALLEY OF BEAUTIES TO THE EASTERN QUEENDOM

1   Of all the Zangzu regions, Danba has the finest weather, and it produces various kinds of fruits, among which guava is the most common. As a result, the guava flower is often referred to as the County Flower.

2   After the Xixia Kingdom established by Dangxiang Qiang in northwest China was destroyed, the Mongol court didn't order the compilation of Xixia history, and most of Xixia's historical documents were either destroyed in the war or disappeared. Consequently, Xixia's history is full of ambiguity. One mystery is the whereabouts of Xixia descendants. A celebrated scholar on Xixia, Li Fanwen, has found linguistic similarities between Ergong, one of the dialects in Danba and neighboring towns, and the dead Xixia language. Extrapolating from Li's findings, the media suggest that the concubines of the king and nobles fled to Danba and produced offspring there.

3   After the national policy of nine years of obligatory education was imple-

mented in Danba, girls receive much more education than they did ten years ago. An increasing number of young women go to other places in Tibetan and Han regions for various jobs and contribute to their families' incomes equally or even more than their male siblings do. Some women in Moluo also get involved in tourism as tour guides, peddlers, and hostesses. However, the effect of these changes on local gender relations and the political status of women remains to be seen.

4  See Nandy 1988; Sinha 1995; Clancy-Smith and Gouda 1998; Glenn 1998; Catherine Hall 2000; Nagel 2003; Ghosh 2004; Ballantyne and Burton 2005.

### 4. THE QUEENDOM AND GRASSROOTS POLITICS

1  See Wasserstrom and Perry 1992; Bianco 2001; O'Brien 2002, 2008; Perry 2002, 2007; Unger 2002; Bernstein and Lü 2003; O'Brien and Li 2006.

2  When asked how they knew these principles, they identified several major sources: TV reports, township and village cadres, other villagers, their literate family members or children. In my observations, however, most villagers don't really understand policies very well. Some of them pointed out that the county and township officials didn't "come down to the village" that much, and even when they came, they would not interact directly with common villagers, nor did they have any intention of propagandizing and explaining the policies. This had to do with the "attitude" issue in the sense that cadres were believed by some villagers not to care much about the peasants' welfare. Older villagers compare present cadres with older ones, and according to them, cadres before the 1980s would spare no effort in propagandizing policies, which kept villagers updated about what was going on at different levels of the state. The lack of connection is also due to language. Most cadres are either Han or Zangzu from other regions who speak different dialects, which makes it difficult for them to convey their ideas to the villagers.

3  The rapid development of Danba County and the province of Sichuan proper has much to do with the Western Development Project initiated by the Chinese government at the turn of the twenty-first century. As a Zangzu region with strategic importance, Ganzi Tibetan Autonomous Prefecture, of which Danba is a part, has received more and more investment in its construction of facilities as well as its economic, and educational development.

4  Suopo Township is composed of three parts or segments: Suopo and Dazhai, both of which are located on the eastern side of the Dadu River, and Pujiaoding on the western side.

5    The old Suopo Bridge has been blocked against automobile and tractor use because of damage from floods in 2004. The county and township governments promised villagers that a new bridge would soon be constructed, but the project did not start until 2008. Construction was slow, and most villagers grew very unhappy about the protracted delay. A rumor spread that the county government had transferred the money for the bridge elsewhere and thus was just performing a show for the villagers because it was concerned about the possibility of "extreme actions."

6    For instance, one villager I know well is famous in Suopo because he has defied local authority, including village heads. He is a fearsome person to many villagers, including elites, because he will not hesitate to take revenge if his interests are threatened. As another example, one village head was a common villager like most others and was elected to this position due to extended kinship ties and his personality: he is patient with and kind to all villagers even though many think he is incompetent. One informant commented, "He is elected . . . he doesn't offend anyone, smiling at everyone all the time . . . villagers feel ashamed if they don't vote for him."

7    For instance, when *Magic Discovery*, a Sichuan TV station program, came to film the relics of the queendom, they designed the scenario of a "big" discovery of the palace remains, presenting it as a chance find by a local herdsman who was looking for his lost livestock, yet all the locals know that the site used to be the queen's palace. This scene became a laughing-stock among locals, and the Suopo native who played the role of the herdsman on TV was ridiculed.

8    As is shown here, the Danba case is not unique in China. In other Tibetan areas, conflicts have intensified as well, though sometimes in a subtler and more inconspicuous way. The tension between many Tibetans, especially monks, and the state has to do with the latter's tightening control over religious and political affairs. The 2008 Tibetan riots were not an accident but were embedded in accumulated enmity and distrust on both sides.

9    See, e.g., Bianco 2001; Perry 2010; O'Brien 2002; Bernstein and Lü 2003.

10    Like Zangzu villagers, the Donfengwa have the right to use or simply "own" their land as a result of the household contract responsibility system, a significant reform of land ownership and use rights initiated in the early 1980s in rural China. In spite of this, the Donfengwa's Zangzu neighbors argue that the Donfengwa are plowing the Zangzu's land instead. As one Zangzu villager asserted, "The Donfengwa are from outside. Where do they get the land?" meaning that the Donfengwa don't have a historical

connection with the land in Suopo and thus their ownership of the land is questionable and unjustifiable.

11  This system refers to the yearly earning distribution principle based on the amount of labor contributed to the collective during the 1950s to the 1970s.

12  The head of one household is a Zangzu cadre in the commune who married a woman from the Han Gang. As a commune cadre, he had a certain amount of influence so that his family was able to stay. The head of another household was running a mill, which Moluo badly needed, and was also allowed to stay with his family.

13  Dongfeng villagers came to the township, threatening to appeal to the county government if the township didn't resolve this issue. The Party secretary answered, "If you want to go, just go. It is none of my business." This angered the villagers, who chased him, intending to beat him. While he was trying to run away, he fell into the river. Many villagers believed that he didn't slip accidentally and that he had no choice but to jump into the river to escape the villagers. Fortunately, he was not injured.

## 5. THE MOLUO TOURISM ASSOCIATION

1  See, e.g., Perry 1994; Forges 1997; Weller 1999, 2005.

2  See White 1993; Weller 1999, 2005; Yijiang Ding 2002; Zheng and Fewsmith 2008.

3  Although Uncle Pema played a major role in building the tourism association, he didn't want to be part of the association directly. According to him, villagers were difficult to deal with, so it was better for him to keep his distance. Moreover, because this association was a "popular association" (*minjian shetuan*) in name, he, as a township cadre, was not supposed to become affiliated.

4  On behalf of the township Party secretary, Uncle Pema gathered the fourteen seniors and two village heads for a discussion of the issues involved in founding a tourism association in Moluo, including membership. According to him, seniors were respected in local culture and also had more public spirit, meaning concern for the welfare of the village. Therefore, they were able to represent the whole village. However, not all seniors were called for the meeting. The fourteen participants were supposedly more keen on village affairs than their peers, most of whom were women.

5  It is said that "Gelindeya" is a name of a local household (in most Tibetan regions, people don't have surnames, but in the rural areas, there is usually a specific name for each household). According to the TV report,

"Gelindeya" literally means "be upright, fair, and amiable." Surprisingly, however, not a single Jiaju local I met had heard of this household name or knew what it meant.

6   In 2005, the Fifth Plenary Session of the Sixteenth Central Committee of the Chinese Communist Party pointed out that in the next five years (2006–10), the New Socialist Countryside Construction project would take on the Party's most important task, enhancing rural reforms in China. This project has five goals: production development (*shengchan fazhan*), prosperous life (*shenghuo fuyu*), folk ethos and civility (*xiangfeng wenmin*), neat and clean village (*cunrong zhengjie*), and democratic management (*guanli minzhu*).

7   See Perry 1985, 1994; Siu 1989; Kelliher 1992; Shu-Min Huang 1998; Weller 1999; Chan, Madsen, and Unger 2009.

8   A great number of works have touched upon the implications of village elections for political participation of the peasants, grassroots democracy and China's democracy as a whole, state-society relations, village power structures, peasant-cadre relationships, and the like (Burns 1988; Weixing Chen 1999; Yijiang Ding 2002; Xiaoqin Guo 2003; Saich 2004; O'Brien and Li 2006; Tan 2006; O'Brien and Han 2009).

9   See Oakes 1998; Davis 2005; Notar 2006; Nyíri 2006; Kolas 2008.

10  I was often impressed with the villagers' emphasis on the importance of *guanxi*. Many villagers are almost superstitious about the power of *guanxi* and argued that one could easily get just about whatever one desired when there was *guanxi*. This obsession with *guanxi* is not very different from the situation in other parts of China (see Mayfair Mei-Hui Yang 1994, Yan 1996).

11  Seniors associations are flourishing in every part of China, including in Danba. This phenomenon is the result of so-called democratic politics in China. On the one hand, it exhibits the increased openness of the Chinese Communist Party, but on the other hand, it shows that the Party favors such quasi–civil associations as seniors associations because of their apolitical nature.

12  This pagoda was said to have been built by Berotsana (Bai Ro Tsa Na), who was dispatched to the Gyarong region in the eighth century due to politico-religious strife at the Tibetan court between supporters of Bon, the indigenous Tibetan religion, and advocates of Buddhism, which was newly introduced from India. According to local legends, Berotsana arrived at Suopo to chase a most powerful but vicious demoness and was finally able to subdue her. As mentioned earlier, the Suopowa's belief in Berotsana is

puzzling in that he was a Buddhist monk who was persecuted by Bon supporters, yet most Suopowa believe in Bon.

13 This is in line with scholars' stance on the hegemonic role of the Chinese state in shaping the agendas and overseeing the activities of civil associations (Weller 1999, 2005; Sujian Guo 2000; Saich 2004).

14 The dynamic relationship between state and society has been foregrounded by some China scholars (see, e.g., Weller 1999, 2005; Zheng and Fewsmith 2008; Perry 2010).

## CONCLUSION

1 I myself was a little surprised by their response. The Suopowa often have a strong Zangzu identity and tend to extol the "greatness" of "Our Zangzu" as opposed to the "hardheaded" Han or other "impure" Gyarongwa. However, when asked about the ethnicity of the township officials—the Party secretary, the township head, the Party vice-secretary, and three vice-heads—most Suopowa would say "I don't know" or "I am not sure." According to some of them, four of these six township officials might be Zangzu due to their local connections (natives of Danba County), but they look like the Han in terms of their behavior or appearance.

2 A parallel example from South Africa is the landless urban San's struggle for identification as indigenous people in order to gain the right to land and other resources. The majority of San who were displaced as a consequence of colonialism and apartheid do not satisfy international organizations' criteria for being considered "authentic" indigenous people and so must adopt an essentialist discourse to "present themselves as largely uncorrupted by historical and political economic context" (Sylvain 2001, 1079) in order to win international and governmental support for their claims. Likewise, in the United States, some claim to be Native Americans in order to obtain certain compensations and benefits.

# GLOSSARY

**Aba Zangzu Qiangzu Zizhizhou** (C) / **Rnga Ba Bod Rigs Dang Chang Rigs Rang Skyong Khul** (T) 阿坝藏族羌族自治州 Aba Tibetan and Qiang Autonomous Prefecture

**baimian shusheng** (C) 白面书生 pallid-faced scholars

**baoshou** (C) 保守 conservative

**Baoxing** (C) 宝兴县 county in Ya'an

**bashe** (T) a circle dance popular in the Kham region

**Beishi** (C) 北史 *History of the Northern Dynasty* (386–581), compiled in the seventh century

**Berotsana** (S) / **Bai Ro Tsa Na** (T) (8th century) one of the first ordained monks in Tibetan Buddhism

**Bon / Bon po** (T) 苯教（苯波教）an indigenous religion in Tibet

**Chamdo** (T) / **Changdu** (C) 昌都 prefecture in the Tibet Autonomous Region

**Chen Duxiu** (C) 陈独秀 (1879–1942) a leading figure in the New Culture Movement and cofounder of the Chinese Community Party

**Chengdu** (C) 成都 capital of Sichuan

**chiku** (C) 吃苦 "eat bitterness"; endure suffering

**Cong Ling** (C) 葱岭 ancient name of the Pamir Mountains in western China and southeastern Central Asia

**cun tianli mie renyu** (C) 存天理, 灭人欲 maintaining the heavenly principle and eradicating the human desire

**cunrong zhengjie** (C) 村容整洁 neat and clean village

**Dadu** (C) 大渡河 major river in Gyarong

**Dajinchuan** (C) 大金川 historical kingdom in Gyarong; today's Jinchuan County, Aba

**Danba** (C) 丹巴县 county in Ganzi

**Dazhai** (C) 大寨片区 one of the three segments of Suopo Township

**diaolou** (C) 碉楼 stone watchtowers widespread in Danba and Gyarong

**diaomin** (C) 刁民 rogue civilians

**difang minzu zhuyi** (C) 地方民族主义 local ethno-nationalism

**Dongfeng** (C) 东风村 village in Suopo Township

**Dongnü Gudu** (C) 东女故都 Ancient Capital of the Eastern Queendom

**Dongnüguo** (C) 东女国 a historically recorded kingdom ruled by women in the Sui and Tang periods

**"Dongnüguo guodu fuchu shuimian"** (C) 东女国国都浮出水面 "The Capital of the Eastern Queendom Comes to Light," a newspaper article

**Dujiangyan** (C) 都江堰 county-level city in Chengdu, Sichuan

**duo minzu de tongyi guojia** (C) 多民族的统一国家 a unified country of diverse ethnic groups

**duoyuan yiti geju** (C) 多元一体格局 "a single unity with multiple cells," an expression coined by Fei Xiaotong, meaning that as indispensable members of multiethnic China, both Han and minorities contribute equally to its unity and diversity

**Fei Xiaotong** (C) 费孝通 (1910–2005) leading Chinese sociologist-anthropologist of the twentieth century

**feiwuzhi wenhua yichan** (C) 非物质文化遗产 intangible cultural heritage

**Ganzi Zangzu Zizhizhou** (C) / **Dkar Mdzes Bod Rigs Rang Skyong Khul** (T) 甘孜藏族羌族自治州 Ganzi Tibetan Autonomous Prefecture

**Gelugpa** (T) 格鲁派 a major school of Tibetan Buddhism

**geshe** (T) 格西 a prestigious degree in the Gelupa School of Tibetan Buddhism

**guanjingtai** (C) 观景台 viewpoint platform

**guanli minzhu** (C) 管理民主 democratic management

**Gyarong / rGyalrong / Rgyal Rong / Shar Rgyal Mo Tsa Ba Rong** (T) 嘉绒 the temperate agricultural area ruled by the queen in the east, or the temperate agricultural area around Mount Murdu in the east

**Gyarongwa** (T) 嘉绒娃 people from Gyarong

**Hantuan** (C) 汉团 Han Gang

**hefa quanyi** (C) 合法权益 lawful rights and interests

**Heishui** (C) 黑水县 county in Aba

**Hongyuan** (C) / **Khyung Mchu** (T) / **Rka Khog Rdzong** (T) 红原县 county in Aba

**huinong zhengce** (C) 惠农政策 preferential policies for peasants

**huodongfei** (C) 活动费 activity fees

**Jiaju** (C) 甲居 village in Danba

**Jialiangyi** (C) 嘉良夷 tribe in northwestern Sichuan in the Sui dynasty, sixth to seventh century

**Jiarong Fengqingjie** (C) 嘉绒风情节 Gyarong Charm Festival

**jiben guoce** (C) 基本国策 basic national policy

**jingji tounao** (C) 经济头脑 economic minds

**jiti shangfang** (C) 集体上访 group appeals to higher authority

*Jiu tangshu* (C) 旧唐书 *Old Tang History*, the earliest extant systematic historical record of the Tang dynasty (618–907), completed in the tenth century

**kaifang** (C) 开放 open

**Kangding** (C) 康定 capital of Ganzi

**kewei** (C) 科委 science commission

**Khyung** (T) a legendary bird in Tibetan tradition

**kordro** (T) a circle dance popular among Tibetans and other ethnic groups

*Lang tuteng* (C) 狼图腾 *Wolf Totem*, a novel by Jiang Rong

**laonian xiehui** (C) 老年协会 seniors association

**li** (C) 礼 proper rites

**Lu Xun** (C) 鲁迅 (1881–1936) one of the most influential writers of the twentieth century in China

**luan gao** (C) 乱搞 casual sexual intercourse

**Luhuo** (C) / **Brag Mgo Rdzong** (T) 炉霍 county in Ganzi

**Maerkang** (C) / **'Bar Khams** (T) 马尔康 capital of Aba

**Meirengu** (C) 美人谷 Valley of Beauties

**Mianning** (C) 冕宁县 county in Liangshan Yi Autonomous Prefecture, Sichuan

**minjian shetuan** (C) 民间社团 popular association

**Minzhu Gaige** (C) 民主改革 Democratic Reform; a political movement oriented toward ethnic minority regions, particularly Tibetan areas, in the late 1950s, that aimed to eradicate feudalism and theocracy, carry out land reforms, and establish the so-called people's democratic regime

**minzhu guanli** (C) 民主管理 democratic administration

**minzhu jiandu** (C) 民主监督 democratic superintendence

**minzhu juece** (C) 民主决策 democratic decision making

**minzhu xuanju** (C) 民主选举 democratic elections

**Moluo** (C) 莫洛 village in Suopo Township, Danba

**Moluo lüyou xiehui** (C) 莫洛旅游协会 Moluo Tourism Association

**Mosuo** (C) 摩梭人 a people with a matrilineal culture residing at Lugu Lake on the Sichuan-Yunnan border

**Murdu / Rgyal Mo Dmu Rdo** (T) 墨尔多 the most sacred mountain in Gyarong

**muxi shizu** (C) 母系氏族 matrilineal clan

**Naxizu** (C) 纳西族 officially identified ethnic group residing in Yunnan

**Ninglang** (C) 宁蒗县 county in Lijiang prefecture, Yunnan

**nongmin** (C) 农民 peasants

**Nüerguo** (C) 女儿国 Women's Country; queendom

**Pujiaoding** (C) 蒲角顶（片区）one of the three segments of Suopo Township

**Qiandiao Zhiguo** (C) 千碉之国 One-Thousand-Watchtower Kingdom

**Qiangzu** (C) 羌族 officially identified ethnic group residing in northwestern Sichuan

**Qianlong** (C) 乾隆 (1711–1799) Qing dynasty emperor

**qiruan paying** (C) 欺软怕硬 bully the weak and fear the strong

**Rangtang** (C) / **'Dzam Thang Rdzong** (T) 壤塘县 county in Aba

**Ranmang** (C) 冉駹 tribe in northwestern Sichuan during the Han dynasty (206 BCE–220 CE)

**rgyal mo** (T) queen

**Rgyal Rong Rgyal Khab Bco Brgyad** (T) Eighteen Kingdoms of Gyarong

**Rgyal Rong skad** (T) / **Jiarong guanhua** (C) 嘉绒官话 "official" language of Gyarong

**Seda** (C) / **Gser Rta Rdzong** (T) 色达县 county in Ganzi

**shar mo rje(?) rgyal po** (T) queen of (or from) the East

**Shehuizhuyi Xinnongcun Jianshe** (C) 社会主义新农村建设 New Socialist Countryside Construction

**sheng fan** (C) 生番 "strange barbarians"; "primitive" minority groups whose cultural practices place them at a great remove from the Han civilization

**shengchan dadui** (C) 生产大队 production brigade

**shengchan fazhan** (C) 生产发展 production development

**shenghuo fuyu** (C) 生活富裕 prosperous life

**Shimian** (C) 石棉县 county in Ya'an

**shu fan** (C) 熟番 "familiar barbarians"; minority groups whose cultural practices are more "civilized" compared to those of "strange barbarians" (*sheng fan*)

**sixiang guannian** (C) 思想观念 mentality; outlook

*Suishu* (C) 隋书 *Book of Sui*, the official history of the Sui dynasty (581–618), compiled in the seventh century

**Suopo** (C) / **Sog Po** (T) 梭坡乡／梭坡片区 township in Danba, Sichuan, as well as one of the three segments of Suopo Township

**Suopowa** (C/T) 梭坡娃 people from Suopo

**suzhi** (C) 素质 personal quality

**suzhi taidi** (C) 素质太低 having very low personal quality

**Tianquan** (C) 天全县 county in Ya'an

**Tianranlin Ziyuan Baohu Gong-cheng** (C) 天然林资源保护工程 Natural Forest Resources Preservation Project

**tianshang diao xianbing** (C) 天上掉馅饼 lit., "pie dropping from the sky"; something obtained by a stroke of luck, usually without effort

**tianxing** (C) 天性 nature; natural instinct

**tinghua** (C) 听话 obedience

**Trisong Detsen** (T) 赤松德赞 eighth-century Tibetan king

**tsampa** (T) 糌粑 roasted barley flour; a Tibetan staple food

**Tsanlha Ngawang** (T) 赞拉·阿旺 (b. 1930) scholar of classical Tibetan and Gyarong language and history

**tusi** (C) 土司 official title conferred on minority chiefs by the court

**weiwen** (C) 维稳 stability maintenance

**Wen Yiduo** (C) 闻一多 (1899–1946) an influential and outspoken poet of the New Cultural Movement

**Wenchuan** (C) 汶川县 county in Aba

**wenming** (C) 文明 civility; manners

**wenrou** (C) 温柔 gentle and soft

**Wuhouci** (C) 武侯祠 district in Chengdu

**xiangfeng wenmin** (C) 乡风文明 folk ethos and civility

**xiangzhang** (C) 乡长 head of a township

**xiao** (C) 孝 filial piety

**Xiaojinchuan** (C) 小金川 kingdom in Gyarong; today's Xiaojin County, Aba

**xiaonong yishi** (C) 小农意识 petty peasant mentality

**xiaoxifu** (C) 小媳妇 "small wife"

**xiejiao** (C) 邪教 vicious cult

*Xin Tangshu* (C) 新唐书 *New Tang History*, revised and modified version of *Old Tang History*, compiled in the eleventh century

**Xishan Zhuqiang** (C) 西山诸羌 Qiang tribes in northwestern Sichuan in the seventh and eighth centuries

**Xixia** (C) 西夏 kingdom in north-western China, eleventh to thirteenth century

**Ya'an** (C) 雅安地区 prefecture-level city in Sichuan

**Yajiang** (C) / **Nyag Chu Kha Rdzong** (T) 雅江县 county in Ganzi

**yiyizhiyi** (C) 以夷制夷 playing off the barbarians against each other

**Yongning** (C) 永宁镇 town in Ninglang County, Yunnan

*Yuanfang youge nüerguo* (C) *The Remote Country of Women* by Bai Hua (b. 1929)

**zang, luan, cha** (C) 脏、乱、差 filthy, disorderly, indecent

**zangmao** (C) "藏猫" Tibetan whore

**Zangzu** (C) 藏族 officially identified Tibetan ethnic group

**zhishi qingnian / zhiqing** (C) 知识青年 "intellectual youth"; youth who were sent down to the countryside to receive an education from poor peasants during the Cultural Revolution

**Zhongguo Lishi Wenhua Mingcun** (C) 中国历史文化名村 Famous Historical and Cultural Village of China

**Zhongguo Zui Meili de Xiangcun** (C) 中国最美丽的乡村 Most Beautiful Countryside in China

**Zhonglu** (C) 中路 township in Danba, Sichuan

**zhongwen qingwu** (C) 重文轻武 esteem literacy and despise martiality

**zhuguan zhuyi** (C) 主观主义 subjectivism

**ziguyilai** (C) 自古以来 since antiquity

**ziyou** (C) 自由 free; autonomous

**zouhun** (C) 走婚 lit., "walking marriage"; informal marriage system among the Mosuo

**zuiren** (C) 罪人 malefactor

**zuzhi yitu** (C) 组织意图 organizational will

# BIBLIOGRAPHY

Anagnost, Ann. 2004. "The Corporeal Politics of Quality (Suzhi)." *Public Culture* 16(2): 189–208.

Anand, Dibyesh. 2007. "Western Colonial Representations of the Other: The Case of Exotica Tibet." *New Political Science* 29(1): 23–42.

Anderson, Benedict. 1991. *Imagined Communities: Reflections on the Origin and Spread of Nationalism.* London and New York: Verso.

Appadurai, Arjun. 1986. "Theory in Anthropology: Center and Periphery." *Comparative Studies in Society and History* 28(2): 356–61.

———, ed. 1996. *Modernity at Large: Cultural Dimensions of Globalization.* Minneapolis: University of Minnesota Press.

Aziz, Barbara Nimri. 1978. *Tibetan Frontier Families: Reflections of Three Generations from D'ing-Ri.* New Delhi: Vikas.

Bai Hua. 1988. *Yuanfang youge nüerguo* [The remote country of women]. Beijing: Renmin Wenxue Chubanshe.

Ballantyne, Tony, and Antoinette M. Burton, eds. 2005. *Bodies in Contact: Rethinking Colonial Encounters in World History.* Durham, NC: Duke University Press.

Baranovitch, Nimrod. 2010. "Others No More: The Changing Representation of Non-Han Peoples in Chinese History Textbooks, 1951–2003." *Journal of Asian Studies* 69(1): 85–122.

Benson, Linda. 1990. *The Ili Rebellion: The Moslem Challenge to Chinese Authority in Xinjiang, 1944-1949.* Armonk, NY: M. E. Sharpe.

Bernstein, Thomas P., and Xiaobo Lü. 2003. *Taxation without Representation in Contemporary Rural China.* Cambridge and New York: Cambridge University Press.

Bhabha, Homi K. 1994. *The Location of Culture.* London and New York: Routledge.

Bianco, Lucien. 2001. *Peasants without the Party: Grass-Roots Movements in Twentieth-Century China.* Armonk, NY: M. E. Sharpe.

Blum, Susan D. 2002. "Margins and Centers: A Decade of Publishing on China's Ethnic Minorities." *Journal of Asian Studies* 61(4): 1287-1310.

Blum, Susan Debra, and Lionel M. Jensen, eds. 2002. *China Off Center: Mapping the Margins of the Middle Kingdom.* Honolulu: University of Hawai'i Press.

Blumenfield, Tami. 2010. *Scenes from Yongning: Media Creation in China's Na Villages.* PhD diss., University of Washington.

Bourdieu, Pierre. 1977. *Outline of a Theory of Practice.* Cambridge and New York: Cambridge University Press.

Bovingdon, Gardner. 2010. *The Uyghurs: Strangers in Their Own Land.* New York: Columbia University Press.

Brag Dgon Pa, Dkon Mchog Bstan Pa Rab Rgyas. 1982. *Mdo smad chos 'byung* [Religious history of Amdo]. Lanzhou: Gansu Minzu Chubanshe.

Brandenberger, David. 2005. "Stalin As Symbol: A Case Study of the Personality Cult and Its Construction." In *Stalin: A New History,* edited by Sarah Davies and James Harris, 249-70. Cambridge: Cambridge University Press.

Brook, Timothy, and B. Michael Frolic, eds. 1997. *Civil Society in China.* Armonk, NY: M. E. Sharpe.

Brown, Melissa J., ed. 1996. *Negotiating Ethnicities in China and Taiwan.* Berkeley: Institute of East Asian Studies, University of California, Berkeley, Center for Chinese Studies.

Brownell, Susan. 1995. *Training the Body for China: Sports in the Moral Order of the People's Republic.* Chicago: University of Chicago Press.

Brownell, Susan, and Jeffrey N. Wasserstrom, eds. 2002. *Chinese Femininities, Chinese Masculinities: A Reader.* Berkeley: University of California Press.

Btsan Lha, Ngag Dbang Tshul Khrims. 1999. "Shilun jiarong zangyu zhong de guzangyu" [On ancient Tibetan in the Gyarong Tibetan language]. *Zhongguo Zangxue* [China Tibetology] (2).

———. 2004. *Zanla Awang Cuocheng lunwenji* [Collection of Btan Lha Ngag Dbang's essays]. Chengdu: Sichuan Minzu Chubanshe.

———. 2007. *Jiarong zangzu de lishi yu wenhua* [History and culture of Gyarong Tibetans]. Chengdu: Sichuan Minzu Chubanshe.

Btsan Lha, Ngag Dbang Tshul Khrims, and Zhang Mianying. 1994. "Jiarong zangxi de lishi yuanyuan ji yishu tezheng" [Historical origin and artistic features of Gyarong Tibetan Opera]. *Sichuan Xiju* [Sichuan Opera] (1).

Bulag, Uradyn Erden. 2002. *The Mongols at China's Edge: History and the Politics of National Unity.* Lanham, MD: Rowman and Littlefield Publishers.

Burns, John P. 1988. *Political Participation in Rural China.* Berkeley: University of California Press.

Cai Hua and Asti Hustvedt. 2001. *A Society without Fathers or Husbands: The Na of China.* New York and Cambridge: Zone Books.

Cai, Yongshun. 2003. "Between State and Peasant: Local Cadres and Statistical Reporting in Rural China." *China Quarterly* 163: 783–805.

Chan, Anita, Richard Madsen, and Jonathan Unger. 2009. *Chen Village: Revolution to Globalization.* Berkeley: University of California Press.

Chen Duxiu. 1915. "Jinri zhi jiaoyu fangzhen" [Today's education principles]. *Xin Qingnian* 1(2).

Chen, Weixing. 1999. *The Political Economy of Rural Development in China, 1978–1999.* Westport, CT: Praeger.

Clancy-Smith, Julia Ann, and Frances Gouda, eds. 1998. *Domesticating the Empire: Race, Gender, and Family Life in French and Dutch Colonialism.* Charlottesville: University Press of Virginia.

Cooper, Frederick, and Ann Laura Stoler, eds. 1997. *Tensions of Empire: Colonial Cultures in a Bourgeois World.* Berkeley: University of California Press.

Crossley, Pamela Kyle. 1997. *The Manchus.* Cambridge, MA: Blackwell Publishers.

Crossley, Pamela Kyle, Helen F. Siu, and Donald S. Sutton, eds. 2006. *Empire at the Margins: Culture, Ethnicity, and Frontier in Early Modern China.* Berkeley: University of California Press.

Dautcher, Jay. 2009. *Down a Narrow Road: Identity and Masculinity in a Uyghur Community in Xinjiang China.* Cambridge, MA: Harvard University Asia Center.

Davis, Sara L. M. 2005. *Song and Silence: Ethnic Revival on China's Southwest Borders.* New York: Columbia University Press.

Deng Tingliang. 1986. "Jiarong zuyuan chutan" [Investigation of the origin of Gyarong Tibetans]. *Xinan Minzu Xueyuan Xuebao* [Journal of the Southwest University for Nationalities] (1).

Dennis, Rutledge M., ed. 2005. *Marginality, Power and Social Structure: Issues in Race, Class, and Gender Analysis.* Amsterdam: Elsevier.

Des Forges, Roger V. 1997. "States, Societies, and Civil Societies in Chinese History." In *Civil Society in China,* edited by T. Brook and B. M. Frolic. Armonk, NY: M. E. Sharpe.

Diamond, Norma. 1988. "The Miao and Poison: Interactions on China's Southwest Frontier." *Ethnology* 27(1): 1–25.

Dietler, Michael. 1994. " 'Our Ancestors the Gauls': Archeology, Ethnic Nationalism, and the Manipulation of Celtic Identity in Modern Europe." *American Anthropologist* 96(3): 584–605.

Ding Chunlian. 2002. "Jiaoshiqun nüxinghua dui xuesheng fazhan de yingxiang ji youhuan" [Impact of the feminization of teachers on students' development]. *Neimenggu Dianda Xuekan* [Journal of the Inner Mongolia Radio and TV University] 4:38–39.

Ding, Yijiang. 2002. *Chinese Democracy after Tiananmen*. New York: Columbia University Press.

Dmu Dge, Bsam Gtan. 1997. *Maoergai Sangmudan quanji disanjuan* [Collections of Dmu Dge Bsam Gtsan: Volume 3]. Xining: Qinghai Minzu Chubanshe.

Dunne, Robert H. 2005. "Marginality: A Conceptual Extension." In *Marginality, Power and Social Structure: Issues in Race, Class, and Gender Analysis*, edited by R. M. Dennis. Amsterdam: Elsevier.

Enloe, Cynthia H. 2000. *Bananas, Beaches and Bases: Making Feminist Sense of International Politics*. Berkeley: University of California Press.

Ewing, Katherine Pratt. 1998. "Crossing Borders and Transgressing Boundaries: Metaphors for Negotiating Multiple Identities." *Ethos* 26(2): 262–67.

Fanon, Frantz. 2008. *Black Skin, White Masks*. New York: Grove Press.

Fei Xiaotong. 1989. "Zhong hua minzu de duoyuan yiti geju" [The Chinese ethnonational landscape of a single unity with multiple cells]. *Beijing Daxue Xuebao* [Journal of Peking University] 4.

Frolic, B. Michael. 1997. "State-Led Civil Society." In *Civil Society in China*, edited by Timothy Brook and B. Michael Frolic. Armonk, NY: M. E. Sharpe.

Gele. 1988. "Gudai zangzu tonghua ronghe xishan zhuqiang yu jiarong zangzu de xingcheng" [On ancient Tibetans' assimilation and incorporation of Xishan Qiang peoples and engendering of Gyarong Tibetans]. *Xizang Yanjiu* [Tibetan Studies] (2).

Ghosh, Durba. 2004. "Gender and Colonialism: Expansion or Marginalization?" *Historical Journal* 47(3): 737–55.

Gladney, Dru C. 1991. *Muslim Chinese: Ethnic Nationalism in the People's Republic*. Cambridge, MA: Council on East Asian Studies, Harvard University.

———. 1994. "Representing Nationality in China: Refiguring Majority/Minority Identities." *Journal of Asian Studies* 53(1): 92–123.

———. 1998. *Ethnic Identity in China: The Making of a Muslim Minority Nationality*. Fort Worth, TX: Harcourt Brace College Publishers.

————. 2004. *Dislocating China: Reflections on Muslims, Minorities, and Other Subaltern Subjects.* Chicago: University of Chicago Press.

Glenn, Evelyn Nakano. 1998. "The Social Construction and Institutionalization of Gender and Race: An Integrative Framework." In *Revisioning Gender,* edited by M. M. Ferree, Judith Lorber, and Beth B. Hess. London: Sage Publications.

Goldstein, Melvyn C., and Cynthia M. Beall. 1990. *Nomads of Western Tibet: The Survival of a Way of Life.* Berkeley: University of California Press.

Goldstein, Melvyn C., and Matthew Kapstein, eds. 1998. *Buddhism in Contemporary Tibet: Religious Revival and Cultural Identity.* Berkeley: University of California Press.

Graburn, N. H. 1983. "Tourism and Prostitution." *Annals of Tourism Research* 10:437–56.

Green, Sarah F. 2005. *Notes from the Balkans: Locating Marginality and Ambiguity on the Greek-Albanian Border.* Princeton, NJ: Princeton University Press.

Guo Shengbo. 2002. "Tangdai Ruoshui Xishan jimi buzu tantao" [Research on the "Ruo-Shui Xishan" tribes under the Tang's control]. *Zhongguo Zangxue* [China Tibetology] (3).

Guo, Sujian. 2000. *Post-Mao China: From Totalitarianism to Authoritarianism?* Westport, CT: Praeger.

Guo, Xiaoqin. 2003. *State and Society in China's Democratic Transition: Confucianism, Leninism, and Economic Development.* New York: Routledge.

Gupta, Akhil. 1992. "Beyond 'Culture': Space, Identity and the Politics of Difference." *Cultural Anthropology* 7(1): 6–23.

Gyatso, Janet. 1987. "Down with the Demoness: Reflections on a Feminine Ground in Tibet." *Tibet Journal* 12(4): 38–53.

Haarh, Erik. 1969. *The Yar-Lun Dynasty.* Copenhagen: Gec Gad's Forlag.

Hall, C. M. 1994. "Nature and Implications of Sex Tourism in South-East Asia." In *Tourism: A Gender Analysis,* edited by V. H. Kinnaird and D. R. Hall. Chichester, UK: John Wiley.

Hall, Catherine, ed. 2000. *Cultures of Empire: Colonizers in Britain and the Empire in the Nineteenth and Twentieth Centuries; A Reader.* New York: Routledge.

Han Li. 2007. "Nanxing ertong chengzhang guocheng zhong nüxinghua xinli qingxiang wenti lixi" [Analysis of the feminized psychological orientation of boys in their socialization]. *Cang Sang* [Vicissitudes] 2:163–65.

Hannerz, Ulf. 1992. *Cultural Complexity: Studies in the Social Organization of Meaning.* New York: Columbia University Press.

Hanson, Allan. 1989. "The Making of the Maori: Culture Invention and Its Logic." *American Anthropologist,* n.s., 91(4): 890–902.

Harrell, Stevan, ed. 1995. *Cultural Encounters on China's Ethnic Frontiers*. Seattle: University of Washington Press.

Harrell, Stevan. 2001. *Ways of Being Ethnic in Southwest China*. Seattle: University of Washington Press.

———. 2007. "L'état, C'est Nous, or We Have Met the Oppressor and He Is Us: The Predicament of Minority Cadres in the PRC." In *The Chinese State at the Borders*, edited by Diana Lary. Vancouver: UBC Press.

Harrell, Stevan, and Li Yongxiang. 2003. "The History of the History of the Yi, Part II." *Modern China* 29 (3): 362–96.

Harrison, Simon. 1999. "Identity As a Scarce Resource." *Social Anthropology* 7(3): 239–51.

He Ping. 2008. "Guojia zaichang xia de funü diwei tisheng yi jianguo chuji de funü jiefang weili" [Elevation of women's status under the "state presence"—A case of women's liberation in the early years of the founding of the PRC]. *Ningbo Shiwei Dangxiao Xuebao* [Journal of the Party School of the CPC Ningbo Municipal Committee].

Heberer, Thomas. 1989. *China and Its National Minorities: Autonomy or Assimilation?* Armonk, NY: M. E. Sharpe.

Hillman, Ben, and Lee-Anne Henfry. 2006. "Macho Minority: Masculinity and Ethnicity on the Edge of Tibet." *Modern China* 32(2): 251–72.

Hobsbawm, Eric. 1994. "Introduction: Inventing Traditions." In *The Invention of Tradition*, edited by E. Hobsbawm and T. Ranger. New York: Cambridge University Press.

Honig, Emily. 2002. "Maoist Mappings of Gender: Reassessing the Red Guards." In *Chinese Femininities, Chinese Masculinities: A Reader*, edited by S. Brownell and J. N. Wasserstrom. Berkeley: University of California Press.

Huang Bufan. 1988. "Chuanxi zangqu de yuyan guanxi" [Language relationships in the Tibetan region of western Sichuan]. *Zhongguo Zangxue* [China Tibetology] (3).

Huang, Shu-Min. 1998. *The Spiral Road: Change in a Chinese Village through the Eyes of a Communist Party Leader*. Boulder, CO: Westview Press.

Huber, Toni. 1999. *The Cult of Pure Crystal Mountain: Popular Pilgrimage and Visionary Landscape in Southeast Tibet*. New York: Oxford University Press.

Hyde, Sandra Theresa. 2001. "Sex Tourism Practices on the Periphery: Eroticizing Ethnicity and Pathologizing Sex on the Lancang." In *China Urban: Ethnographies of Contemporary Culture*, edited by N. N. Chen. Durham, NC: Duke University Press.

Jacques, Guillaume. 2008. *Jiarongyu yanjiu* [A study of the Rgyalrong language]. Beijing: Minzu Chubanshe.

Jia, Xiaofeng. 2007. *Zangqu tusi zhidu yanjiu* [Research on the *tusi* system in Tibetan regions]. PhD diss., Lanzhou University.

Jiang, Rong. 2008. *Wolf Totem*. Translated by Howard Goldblatt. New York: Penguin Press.

Kapchan, Deborah A., and Pauline Turner Strong. 1999. "Theorizing the Hybrid." *Journal of American Folklore* 112(445): 239–53.

Karmay, Samten. 1996. "The Cult of Mount Murdo in Gyalrong." *Kailash* 18(1–2): 1–16.

Kaup, Katherine Palmer. 2000. *Creating the Zhuang: Ethnic Politics in China*. Boulder, CO: L. Rienner.

Kelliher, Daniel Roy. 1992. *Peasant Power in China: The Era of Rural Reform, 1979–1989*. New Haven, CT: Yale University Press.

Kinkley, Jeffrey C. 1987. *The Odyssey of Shen Congwen*. Stanford, CA: Stanford University Press.

Kolas, Ashild. 2008. *Tourism and Tibetan Culture in Transition: A Place Called Shangrila*. New York: Routledge.

Kolas, Ashild, and Monika P. Thowsen. 2005. *On the Margins of Tibet: Cultural Survival on the Sino-Tibetan Frontier*. Seattle: University of Washington Press.

Korom, Frank J. 1994. "Memory, Innovation and Emergent Ethnicities: The Creolization of an Indo-Trinidadian Performance." *Diaspora* 3(2): 135–55.

Li Qiuling and Huang Yuyun. 2004. "Dui woguo chudeng jiaoyu jiaoshi nüxinghua xianxiang de sisuo" [Thoughts on the "feminization" of primary school teachers in China]. *Shiyou Jiaoyu* [Petroleum Education] 6:106–8.

Li Shaoming. 1980. "Tangdai Xishan zhuqiang kaolue" [Investigation of Xishan Qiang peoples in the Tang]. *Sichuan Daxue Xuebao* [Journal of Sichuan University] (1).

Li Tao and Li Xinyou, eds. 1995. *Jiarong zangzu yanjiu ziliao congbian* [Collection of Gyarong Tibetan research materials]. Chengdu: Sichuan Zangxue Yanjiusuo.

Li Xingyou. 1995. "Jiarongyu yu zangyu guanxici fenxi" [Analysis of relatives in Gyarong and Tibetan languages]. In *Jiarong zangzu yanjiu ziliao congbian* [Collection of Gyarong Tibetan research materials], edited by Li Tao and Li Xinyou. Chengdu: Sichuan Zangxue Yanjiusuo.

Liang Yong, Li Bai, and Huang Lin. 2006. "Xiaoxue zhonggao nianji nanhai nüxinghua qingxiang de yanjiu" [Investigation of the feminized tendency of boys in the medium and higher grades of primary schools]. *Fuyang Shifan Xueyuan Xuebao* [Journal of Fuyang Normal College] (4): 96–98.

Lin Junhua. 2006a. *Danba meinü* [Danba beauties]. Chengdu: Tiandi Chubanshe.

———. 2006b. "Danbaxian yuyan wenhua ziyuan diaocha" [Investigation of language and cultural resources of Danba County]. *Kangding Minzu Shifan Gaodeng Zhuanke Xuexiao Xuebao* [Journal of Kangding Nationality Teachers' College] 15(5).

Lin Xiangrong. 1993. *Jiarongyu yanjiu* [Study of Gyarong language]. Chengdu: Sichuan Minzu Chubanshe.

Lindholm, Charles. 2008. *Culture and Authenticity.* Malden, MA: Blackwell Publishers.

Linnekin, Jocelyn S. 1990. "Cultural Invention and the Dilemma of Authenticity." *American Anthropologist*, n.s., 93(2): 446–49.

Litzinger, Ralph A. 2000. *Other Chinas: The Yao and the Politics of National Belonging.* Durham, NC: Duke University Press.

Louie, Kam. 2002. *Theorising Chinese Masculinity: Society and Gender in China.* Cambridge: Cambridge University Press.

Luo Changpei and Fu Maoxun. 1954. "Guonei shaoshu minzu yuyan wenzi de gaikuang" [Introduction to minority oral and written languages in China]. *Zhongguo Yuwen* [Chinese Languages] (21).

Ma Changshou. 1944. "Jiarong minzu shehuishi" [Social history of Gyarong people]. *Minzuxue Yanjiu Jikan* [Ethnic Studies Series] 4.

Ma Chengfu. 2006. "Jinchuan nüerguo jiqi wenhua yisu tanmi" [Exploration of the Eastern Queendom in Jinchuan and its cultural heritage]. *Xizang Yishu Yanjiu* [Tibetan Arts Studies] 82(4).

MacCannell, Dean. 1976. *The Tourist: A New Theory of the Leisure Class.* New York: Schocken Books.

Mackerras, Colin. 1994. *China's Minorities: Integration and Modernization in the Twentieth Century.* Hong Kong and New York: Oxford University Press.

———. 2003. *China's Ethnic Minorities and Globalisation.* London: Routledge-Curzon.

Makley, Charlene E. 2003. "Gendered Boundaries in Motion: Space and Identity on the Sino-Tibetan Frontier." *American Ethnologist* 30(4): 597–619.

———. 2007. *The Violence of Liberation: Gender and Tibetan Buddhist Revival in Post-Mao China.* Berkeley: University of California Press.

Mueggler, Erik. 2001. *The Age of Wild Ghosts: Memory, Violence, and Place in Southwest China.* Berkeley: University of California Press.

———. 2002. "Dancing Fools: Politics of Culture and Place in a 'Traditional Nationality Festival'." *Modern China* 28(1): 3–38.

Nagel, Joane. 2003. *Race, Ethnicity, and Sexuality: Intimate Intersections, Forbidden Frontiers.* New York: Oxford University Press.

Nandy, Ashis. 1988. *The Intimate Enemy: Loss and Recovery of Self under Colonialism.* New Delhi and New York: Oxford University Press.

Notar, Beth E. 2006. *Displacing Desire: Travel and Popular Culture in China.* Honolulu: University of Hawai'i Press.

Nyíri, Pál. 2006. *Scenic Spots: Chinese Tourism, the State, and Cultural Authority.* Seattle: University of Washington Press.

Oakes, Tim. 1997. "Ethnic Tourism in Rural Guizhou: Sense of Place and the Commerce of Authenticity." In *Tourism, Ethnicity, and the State in Asian and Pacific Societies*, edited by M. Picard and R. E. Wood. Honolulu: University of Hawai'i Press.

———. 1998. *Tourism and Modernity in China.* London and New York: Routledge.

———. 2005. "Land of Living Fossils: Excavating Cultural Prestige in China's Periphery." In *Locating China: Space, Place and Popular Culture*, edited by J. Wang. London and New York: Routledge.

———, ed. 2007. "Welcome to Paradise! A Sino-American Joint Venture Project." In *China's Transformations: The Stories beyond the Headlines*, edited by T. Weston and L. Jenson. Lanham, MD: Rowman and Littlefield.

O'Brien, Kevin J. 2002. "Collective Action in the Chinese Countryside." *China Journal* 48: 139–54.

———, ed. 2008. *Popular Protest in China.* Cambridge, MA: Harvard University Press.

O'Brien, Kevin J., and Rongbin Han. 2009. "Path to Democracy? Assessing Village Elections in China." *Journal of Contemporary China* 18(60): 359–78.

O'Brien, Kevin J., and Lianjiang Li. 2006. *Rightful Resistance in Rural China.* New York: Cambridge University Press.

Ortner, Sherry B. 1999. *Life and Death on Mt. Everest: Sherpas and Himalayan Mountaineering.* Princeton, NJ: Princeton University Press.

Peng Zhiyan. 2003. "Shilun Qianlong pingding Jinchuan zhi yingxiang" [On the impacts of the Qianlong emperor's subduing of Jinchuans]. *Xizang Yanjiu* [Tibetan Studies] (1).

Perry, Elizabeth J. 1985. "Rural Violence in Socialist China." *China Quarterly* 103: 414–40.

———. 1994. "Trends in the Study of Chinese Politics: State-Society Relations." *China Quarterly* 139: 704–13.

———. 2002. *Challenging the Mandate of Heaven: Social Protest and State Power in China.* Armonk, NY: M. E. Sharpe.

———. 2006. *Patrolling the Revolution: Worker Militias, Citizenship, and the Modern Chinese State.* Lanham, MD: Rowman and Littlefield.

———. 2007. "Studying Chinese Politics: Farewell to Revolution?" *China Journal* 57: 1–22.

———. 2010. "Popular Protest: Playing by the Rules." In *China Today, China Tomorrow: Domestic Politics, Economy, and Society*, edited by J. Fewsmith. Lanham, MD: Rowman and Littlefield.

Perry, Elizabeth J., and Merle Goldman, eds. 2007. *Grassroots Political Reform in Contemporary China*. Cambridge, MA: Harvard University Press.

Prakash, Gyan. 1994. "Subaltern Studies as Postcolonial Criticism." *American Historical Review* 99(5): 1475–90.

Pratt, Mary L. 1991. "Arts of the Contact Zone." *Profession* 91: 33–40.

Pruitt, Deborah, and Suzanne LaFont. 1995. "For Love and Money: Romance Tourism in Jamaica." *Annals of Tourism Research* 22(2): 422–40.

Qu Aitang. 1984. "Jiarongyu gaikuang" [Introduction to the Gyarong language]. *Minzu Yuwen* [Ethnic Languages] (2).

———. 1990. "Jiarongyu de fangyan—fangyan huafen yu yuyan shibie" [Dialects of the Gyarong Language: Dialect Classification and Language Identification]. *Minzu Yuwen* [Ethnic Languages] (4/5).

Quedan. 1995. *Jiarong zangzu shizhi* [Historical records of Gyarong Tibetans]. Beijing: Minzu Chubanshe.

Rockhill, William Woodville. 1891. *The Land of the Lamas*. London: Longmans, Green, and Co.

Rosaldo, Renato. 1993. *Culture and Truth: The Remaking of Social Analysis*. Boston: Beacon Press.

Rossabi, Morris, ed. 2004. *Governing China's Multiethnic Frontiers*. Seattle: University of Washington Press.

Rudelson, Justin Jon. 1997. *Oasis Identities: Uyghur Nationalism along China's Silk Road*. New York: Columbia University Press.

Ryan, Chris, and Colin Michael Hall. 2001. *Sex Tourism: Marginal People and Liminalities*. London and New York: Routledge.

Ryan, Chris, and Rachel Kinder. 1996. "Sex, Tourism, and Sex Tourism: Fulfilling Similar Needs?" *Tourism Management* 17(7): 507–18.

Saich, Tony. 2004. *Governance and Politics of China*. Basingstoke, UK, and New York: Palgrave Macmillan.

Schein, Louisa. 1997. "Gender and Internal Orientalism in China." *Modern China* 23(1): 69–98.

———. 2000. *Minority Rules: The Miao and the Feminine in China's Cultural Politics*. Durham, NC: Duke University Press.

Schwartz, Ronald D. 1994. *Circle of Protest: Political Ritual in the Tibetan Uprising*. New York: Columbia University Press.

Scott, James C. 2009. *The Art of Not Being Governed: An Anarchist History of Upland Southeast Asia*. New Haven, CT: Yale University Press.

Shi Shuo. 2001. *Zangzu zuyuan ji zangdong guwenming* [The origin of Tibetans and the ancient civilization of east Tibet]. Chengdu: Sichuan Minzu Chubanshe.

———. 2009a. "*Jiutangshu* Dongnüguo zhuan suoji chuanxi gaoyuan nüguo de shiliao cuanluan ji xiangguan wenti" [On the jumbled historical materials about the Women's Country in the west Sichuan Plateau in the "Records of the Eastern Queendom" in the *Old Tang History*]. *Zhongguo Zangxue* [China Tibetology] (3).

———. 2009b. "Nüguo shi Supi ma lun Nüguo yu Supi zhi chayi ji Nüguo ji Supi shuo zhi yuanqi" [Is Women's Country the Same as Sum-Pa(Supi)?: On the difference between Women's Country and Supi and the origin of the claim of Women's Country as Supi]. *Xizang Yanjiu* [Tibetan Studies] (3).

Shih, Chuan-Kang. 2010. *Quest for Harmony: The Moso Traditions of Sexual Union and Family Life*. Stanford, CA: Stanford University Press.

Sinha, Mrinalini. 1995. *Colonial Masculinity: The "Manly Englishman" and the "Effeminate Bengali" in the Late Nineteenth Century*. Manchester, UK: Manchester University Press.

Siu, Helen F. 1989. *Agents and Victims in South China: Accomplices in Rural Revolution*. New Haven, CT: Yale University Press.

Sneath, David. 2000. *Changing Inner Mongolia: Pastoral Mongolian Society and the Chinese State*. Oxford and New York: Oxford University Press.

Spence, Jonathan D. 1981. *The Gate of Heavenly Peace: The Chinese and Their Revolution, 1895–1980*. New York: Viking Press.

Spitzer, Nicholas R. 2003. "Monde Créole: The Cultural World of French Louisiana Creoles and the Creolization of World Cultures." *Journal of American Folklore* 116 (459): 57–72.

Starr, S. Frederick, ed. 2004. *Xinjiang: China's Muslim Borderland*. Armonk, NY: M. E. Sharpe.

Stein, Rolf Alfred. 1972. *Tibetan Civilization*. Stanford, CA: Stanford University Press.

Stoler, Ann Laura. 1989. "Making Empire Respectable: The Politics of Race and Sexual Morality in Twentieth-Century Colonial Cultures." *American Ethnologist* 4(3): 634–60.

Sun Hongkai. 1983. "Liujiang liuyu de minzu yuyan jiqi xishu fenlei" [Minority languages in the Ranges of Six Rivers and their classification]. *Minzu Xuebao* [Journal for Ethnic Groups] (3).

Sun, Jackson. 2000. "Parallelisms in the Verb Morphology of Sidaba Rgyalrong and Guanyinqiao in Rgyalrongic." *Language and Linguistics* 1(1): 161–90.

Sun Yunxiao. 1993. "Xialingying de jiaoliang" [Contest at the summer camp]. *Duzhe* [Readers] (11).

Sun Yunxiao, Li Wendao, and Zhao Xiao. 2010. *Zhengjiu nanhai* [Save boys]. Beijing: Zuojia Chubanshe.

Sylvain, Renee. 2001. "'Land, Water, and Truth': San Identity and Global Indigenism." *American Anthropologist* 104(4): 1074–85.

Tan, Qingshan. 2006. *Village Elections in China: Democratizing the Countryside.* New York: Edwin Mellen Press.

Teng, Emma. 2004. *Taiwan's Imagined Geography: Chinese Colonial Travel Writing and Pictures, 1683–1895.* Cambridge, MA.: Harvard University Asia Center.

Thomas, Frederick William. 1957. *Ancient Folk-Literature from North-Eastern Tibet.* Berlin: Abhandlungen der Deutschen Akademie der Wissenschaften zu Berlin.

Titus, Paul, ed. 1996. *Marginality and Modernity: Ethnicity and Change in Postcolonial Balochistan.* New York: Oxford University Press.

Tobin, Joseph J., David Y. H. Wu, and Dana H. Davidson. 1989. *Preschool in Three Cultures: Japan, China, and the United States.* New Haven, CT: Yale University Press.

Truong, Thanh-Dam. 1990. *Sex, Money, and Morality: Prostitution and Tourism in Southeast Asia.* London and Atlantic Highlands, NJ: Zed Books.

Tsing, Anna Lowenhaupt. 1993. *In the Realm of the Diamond Queen: Marginality in an Out-of-the-Way Place.* Princeton, NJ: Princeton University Press.

Tucci, Giuseppe. 1956. *Preliminary Report on Two Scientific Expeditions in Nepal.* Rome: Istituto Italiano per il Medio ed Estremo Oriente.

Unger, Jonathan. 2002. *The Transformation of Rural China.* Armonk, NY: M. E. Sharpe.

Wagner, Roy. 1975. *The Invention of Culture.* Englewood Cliffs, NJ: Prentice-Hall.

Walsh, Eileen Rose. 2005. "From Nü Guo to Nü'er Guo: Negotiating Desire in the Land of the Mosuo." *Modern China* 31(4): 448–86.

Wang Haiying. 2007. "Xiaoxue Jiaoshi nüxinghua zhongguo jiaoyu de qianzai weiji" ["Feminization" of primary school teachers: The latent crisis of education in China]. *Qiyejia Tiandi* [Entrepreneur World] 3:172.

Wang Huailin. 2006. *Xunzhao Dongnüguo* [Searching for the Eastern Queendom]. Chengdu: Sichuan Minzu Chubanshe.

Wang Xianhua. 2003. "Nanhai jiaoyu dangxin nüxinghua" [Be aware of feminization in boys' education]. *Jiating Keji* [Family Science and Technology] 12.

Wang Yao. 1987. "Zangyu mig zi gudu kao jianlun zangyu shengdiao de fasheng yu fazhan" [Investigation of the ancient pronunciation of a Tibetan word—"mig"—and of engendering and developing tones in Tibetan]. *Minzu Yuwen* [Ethnic Languages] (4).

Wasserstrom, Jeffrey N., and Elizabeth J. Perry, eds. 1992. *Popular Protest and Political Culture in Modern China: Learning from 1989.* Boulder, CO: Westview Press.

Weller, Robert P. 1999. *Alternate Civilities: Democracy and Culture in China and Taiwan*. Boulder, CO: Westview Press.

———, ed. 2005. *Civil Life, Globalization, and Political Change in Asia: Organizing between Family and State*. London and New York: Routledge.

Weller, Robert P. 2006. *Discovering Nature: Globalization and Environmental Culture in China and Taiwan*. Cambridge: Cambridge University Press.

Weller, Robert P., and Scott E. Guggenheim, eds. 1982. *Power and Protest in the Countryside: Studies of Rural Unrest in Asia, Europe, and Latin America*. Durham, NC: Duke University Press.

White, Gordon. 1993. *Riding the Tiger: The Politics of Economic Reform in Post-Mao China*. Stanford, CA: Stanford University Press.

Wu Wenyu. 2008. "Youeryuan ji xiaoxue dinianji jiaoyu yu nanhai nüxinghua" [Education at kindergartens and lower grades of primary schools and boys' feminization]. *Jixu Jiaoyu Yanjiu* [Continuing Education Research] 12:129–30.

Wu Yong. 2001. "Sichuan faxian Xixia houyi" [Xixia descendants are found in Sichuan]. *Renmin Ribao Haiwaiban* [Overseas Version of *The People's Daily*, May 10].

Xueniu. 2003. *Danba fengqing* [Danba charm]. Beijing: Sanxia Chubanshe.

Yan, Yunxiang. 1996. *The Flow of Gifts: Reciprocity and Social Networks in a Chinese Village*. Stanford, CA: Stanford University Press.

Yang, Dali L. 1996. *Calamity and Reform in China: State, Rural Society, and Institutional Change since the Great Leap Famine*. Stanford, CA: Stanford University Press.

Yang Erche Namu and Christine Mathieu. 2003. *Leaving Mother Lake: A Girlhood at the Edge of the World*. Boston: Little, Brown.

Yang Jiaming and Yang Yi. 2004. *Qiandiao zhiguo Danba* (Thousand-watchtower kingdom—Danba). Chengdu: Bashu Shushe.

Yang, Mayfair Mei-Hui. 1994. *Gifts, Favors, and Banquets: The Art of Social Relationships in China*. Ithaca, NY: Cornell University Press.

Young, Robert. 1995. *Colonial Desire: Hybridity in Theory, Culture, and Race*. London and New York: Routledge.

Zeng Xianjiang. 2004. "Jiarong yanjiu zongshu" [A survey of Gyarong Tibetan studies]. *Xizang Yanjiu* [Tibetan Studies] (2).

Zhao, Suisheng, ed. 2000. *China and Democracy: The Prospect for a Democratic China*. New York: Routledge.

Zheng, Yongnian, and Joseph Fewsmith. 2008. *China's Opening Society: The Non-state Sector and Governance*. London and New York: Routledge.

# INDEX

Except for certain key terms, those that appear in the notes are not indexed.